# SMART GOLF

# SMART GOLF

**A STUDY OF THE MENTAL AND EMOTIONAL SIDE OF THE GAME OF GOLF**

by

CHARLES F. KEMP, Ph.D

**TEXAS CHRISTIAN UNIVERSITY**

**1974**

**BRANCH-SMITH, INC.**
**Fort Worth, Texas**
**75101**

We express our appreciation for permission to include in this work statements from many sources, credits for which are shown on page 146.


Library of Congress Catalog Card No. 74-82856
ISBN 87706-057-6
Printed in the United States of America
**Composition and Layout by**
**Four Graphics, Inc.**

# Foreword by Byron Nelson

"I enjoyed reading your book *Smart Golf.* The right mental approach is smart golf. It will improve your score and make the game more fun."

Byron Nelson

"I am delighted to act as publisher for the first edition of *Smart Golf.* It is a masterpiece and a great contribution to the golf-world."

Hugh Wolfe
Stephenville, Texas

# Acknowledgments

A particular word of appreciation should be expressed to certain persons whose encouragement and assistance has been of great help. First of all, Mr. Hugh Wolfe of Stephenville, Texas, read the entire manuscript. He is a former All-American half-back at the University of Texas and an excellent amateur golfer. He was very encouraging; in fact, without his support and assitance it probably would never have been completed.

I next asked Dr. Granville Walker, who was then the pastor of University Christian Church in Fort Worth, to read the material. He is very knowledgable about golf and golf literature. He too felt it had real merit.

Having secured the opinion of both a low and high handicapper it was felt that a professional judgment was needed. Mr. Byron Nelson, one of the golf immortals, was kind enough, in the midst of a very busy schedule, to read the entire manuscript and to encourage me as to the value of the project. For that I am very grateful.

Some mention should be made of two teaching pros. Mr. Roland Harper, head pro at Colonial Country Club in Fort Worth, home of the well known Colonial National Tournament, has been my friend for many years. Mr. Raymond Gafford is the head pro at the Ridglea Country Club in Fort Worth, my home pro. I have had innumerable conversations with both of these men about all aspects of golf. Both are excellent teaching pros and have taught me much about the fundamentals and subtleties of the golf swing.

I should also express my appreciation to the many golfers whose experiences and statements provided the basis for the material that is included. In each case where a quote appears we have made every effort to give full credit both to the golfer and to the publisher.

Mr. Al Panzera, awards winning sports photographer for The Fort Worth Star-Telegram, supplied most of the photographs used in this book.

To Jim

# Contents

# Illustrations

# INTRODUCTION:

## Some Questions and Answers about this Volume

There has been so much published on golf in recent years that any new volume needs to have certain questions answered about it before it can justify a reader's time or expense—especially one written by a minister who also happens to be a psychologist.

**What is the book about?** It is about the mental and emotional sides of golf. It is a study of the thoughts and attitudes that the world's greatest golfers, past and present, felt contributed to their success.

**What are the sources?** The sources for information are the golfers themselves. It is a collection and a summary of the experiences and statements of the world's greatest golfers.

**Where were these statements found?** In books, magazine articles, sometimes from newspaper or television interviews. More than seventy volumes written by famous golfers were carefully read and studied. All of the issues of *Golf Magazine*, *Golf Digest* and *Golf and Club* for the last ten years were read and documented, as well as other journals which carry feature articles on golf, such as *Sports Illustrated, Sporting News,* etc. Every effort was made to make the research as thorough and as complete as possible.

**What golfers were included?** All successful golfers who made statements about the mental or psychological side of golf. Obviously this included more touring pros than anything else, although statements of teaching pros and successful amateurs are included when they are pertinent. Some golfers have published more than others; some are interviewed more than others; hence quotes and illustrations from their careers are easier to obtain.

**What period in golfing history is included?** From Harry Vardon to the present. Prior to Vardon it is difficult to secure quotes. Golfers of the period from Jones through Hagen and Sarazen and down to Nelson and Hogan are recent enough that much material is available. The recent increase in interest in golf, the very rapid expansion in publication about golf and the advent of television interviews make the thoughts and experiences of contemporary golfers easy to obtain. With the present-day group the question is not one of getting illustrative material but of selecting the material to be used.

**Hasn't this been done before?** No, not in the way that is has been done here. There have been a lot of statements about the importance of the mental side of golf. There have been several articles and even a few books on the psychology of golf. This is the first attempt to gather together illustrations and statements of those who have actually been successful at golf, to organize them, and to put them all in one volume.

**By what authority is it written?** This is a fair question. The subject of this volume deals with two topics and how they relate to each other: mental attitudes and golf. Both by training and experience I have dealt extensively with the former. I am a licensed psychologist in the state of Texas and an ordained minister. In both fields one's primary focus is on people's thoughts and attitudes. For the last sixteen years I have been on the faculty of a major university, Texas Christian University, where research is one of my responsibilities. In research my task is the organization, evaluation and presentation of data. This is my justification for presenting material on the psychology of golf. This does not depend on my ability as an athlete but my ability as a research scholar. I have attempted to evaulate the thoughts and attitudes of those who have demonstrated skill as athletes. I have made an honest effort to be as thorough as possible, to collect, organize and interpret their experiences as best I can. On the other side of the picture, as a golfer, I am an avid fan, I love the game and my handicap varies from a 2 to a 6.

**What is its purpose?** The purpose or purposes of this study are two-fold. First is to gather together in one volume the experiences and statements of successful golfers about the mental and emotional aspects of the game. This is of interest both from a psychological and from an athletic point of view. It should help the general public or the average fan to understand the game better and to appreciate its heroes a bit more. A second purpose is more practical. It is our firm belief, as stated above, that a knowledge of the thoughts and attitudes of successful golfers will significantly help anyone lower his or her score if he will apply the principles outlined here. It has proven so in my own case.

**Why was it written?** It began as a hobby. I have always been interested in human achievement in any field. There is something inspiring about a person who selects an area of interest or service and prepares himself to the best of his ability and utilizes his talents to the maximum of his potential. This is true whether it is in the field of science, scholarship, statesmanship or religion. It is also true in athletics. I have always admired the great athletes in general, and great golfers in particular.

Some years ago I became interested in statements about the significance of mental attitudes in attaining such achievements. Then I began to collect and compare these statements. The next step was to search for them. It was then I began to explore the golfing literature, past and present, to watch the action in the tournaments with a new perspective, to listen with a new interest to post tournament interviews, to read accounts of tournaments in the golfing journals with a new purpose.

Studying the experiences of successful golfers, analyzing their statements soon became not only interesting but, at times, exciting. It was then I felt I was accumulating some psychological and golfing data that was both interesting and significant.

Much of it seemed to fall into certain areas or categories. Some of it was repetitious. Much was common to all golfers. All underlined the same truth. This is one of the most important factors of the game.

This was so interesting to me that I thought it might be of interest to others. I showed it to some friends who encouraged me to have it published. It still seemed presumptuous for a professor in a university to write a book on golf, but, when Byron Nelson himself read the manuscript and said the material was sound, I felt I was on solid ground, or to use a more appropriate analogy I felt I was in the fairway.

The study of the thoughts and attitudes of successful golfers has been such a source of real pleasure to me that I sincerely hope it will be of value to others who will find here clues to those thoughts and attitudes that will lower their scores and help them to enjoy the game even more than they do now.

**Charles F. Kemp, Ph.D.**
**Texas Christian University**
**Fort Worth, Texas**

# 1

# The Intangibles Of Golf

The game of golf was born in the city of St. Andrews in northern Scotland several hundred years ago. On the first page of a history of that famous city one finds this phrase: "This fascinating, infuriating, this amazing, absorbing game of golf."[1] One thing that makes the game so "fascinating", at times "infuriating", often "amazing", but always "absorbing" is the fact that golf, more than any other sport, is influenced by one's thoughts and attitudes.

The great Ben Hogan said the game is more psychological than physical. Arnold Palmer frequently quotes his golf professional father who said, "Ninety percent of golf is played from the shoulders up." Gary Player said, "What you think" is the most determining factor of what you do on the golf course. Paul Runyan, recognized as one of the most competent teachers and analysts of the game, said he thought that golf was made up of about 40 percent technical skills and 60 percent mental and emotional stability.[2] Sam Snead said, ". . .if your mind is out of kilter, ten thousand lessons and a team of mules won't help you."[3] Julius Boros said one's mental attitudes must become as grooved as his swing. Such quotations could be continued indefinitely. On this theme there seems to be common agreement.

We wanted to determine if there was any agreement as to what the common thoughts and attitudes of successful golfers were. Is there any set of thoughts and attitudes which can be considered fundamental—such as keeping the head steady and the left arm straight—on the mechanical side of golf? We found that there is pretty common agreement on many points and some differences on others. We have tried to report both. After such an investigation we are quite convinced, as stated earlier, that, given the fundamentals, it is the intangibles that count.

We recognize that there is considerable overlapping in some of these discussions. It is hard to separate "patience" and "perseverance", for example. It is a fine line between "visualization" and "concentration", yet each is a bit different from the other. Some concepts, such as "confidence", actually apply to almost every topic discussed.

Jim Fleck, a teaching pro from Cincinnati, Ohio, and a member of Golf Digest instruction panel said in an article that he didn't think the average golfer had any idea how important a positive mental attitude was and that he felt one of the most important things the average golfer could learn was both the importance of the mind in golf and how it could be used.[4] That's what we hope the rest of these pages will do. We not only want to make people aware of the importance of mental attitudes in golf, but in describing how others have done this, it should make people aware of how they can do it too.

The intangibles in sport have never been adequately studied. Anyone connected with athletics, either as a spectator or as a competitor, knows that they exist and that they exert a powerful influence. In any contest, given two teams or two individuals of equal ability—the intangibles will determine the outcome every time; in fact, they may determine the outcome if the contestants are of unequal ability. Many a person has become an effective athlete and excelled men of

**Golf is a game of the emotions—it has many disappointments**

**Sikes, Douglas, Smith**

greater natural talent simply because he used the intangibles well.

Tom Nieporte and Don Sauers conducted a survey of fifty leading professional golfers. They asked them what they considered to be more important, the mechanical side of golf or the psychological side. The pros voted for the psychological three to one.(5)

Interestingly enough, however, although the pros all stress the importance of the intangibles, when they write or publish they deal with the mechanics of the game. Anyone who has made a study of the golfing literature knows of the infinite detail with which they discuss the grip, the stance, the back-swing, the downswing, the follow through, the various trouble shots, etc. All of this has to do with the mechanics of golf. Usually there are references to such things as concentration, relaxation, and confidence, but they are limited in comparison.

When one reads the books written by the well-known professionals he finds that the number of pages given to the mechanics and fundamentals outnumbers the number of pages given to the mental aspect of the game almost 8 to 1. Yet they all agree that it is the intangibles that make the difference.* (see footnote at end of chapter) This aspect of the game has not been studied and documented as much as the other—and for good reason. One can observe the mechanics of the swing, but one cannot observe the attitudes inside a person's mind.

We would not minimize the importance of mechanics or of fundamentals. That cannot be overemphasized, especially for the beginner; in fact, for the beginner, they are probably more important than anything else. We will stress that more in a later chapter. If a person's grip is wrong, if his swing has flaws, he will not produce consistent results no matter what his thoughts or attitudes. Once he has mastered the fundamentals fairly well, then it is the intangibles that make the difference.

What are these intangibles that are so important? They are

**Golf is a game of the emotions—it has many thrills and satisfactions**
**Weiskopf, Littler, Cole**

many. Patience and persistence in preparation. A willingness to make extra effort. The pursuit of excellence. A desire to win. The capacity to remain calm under pressure. The courage and perseverence to continue in spite of discouragement. The capacity to control one's emotions. The ability to relax and be alert at the same time. The ability to concentrate in a positive manner. Faith in one's self. Billy Casper summarized them as the four "D's" of golf: desire, discipline, determination and dedication. Arnold Palmer speaks of the four "C's" of golf: concentration, confidence, competitive urge, and capacity for enjoyment.[(6)] Bob Toski also speaks of the three C's of golf—he says they are, confidence, concentration and composure, all of which are necessary for good golf.

*After completing this manuscript and re-reading the material it occurred to me that I should have documented such a statement. I had originally written it 10 to 1, primarily as an estimate based on my reading. To check my observation I selected six widely read instructional books by six of the greatest golfers of all:

Tommy Armour: *How to Play Your Best Golf All the Time*
Julius Boros: *How to Play Golf With an Effortless Swing*
Ben Hogan: *The Modern Fundamentals of Golf*
Cary Middlecoff: *Master Guide to Golf*
Arnold Palmer: *My Game and Yours*
Gary Player: *Gary Player's Golf Secrets*

I felt they were fairly typical. They totaled 998 pages of instruction. I counted 161 pages devoted to the psychological side of golf. Allowing for the fact that there were occasional references to attitudes in sections dealing with the mechanics, I changed my estimate to 8 to 1.

(1) ROBERTSON: *St. Andrews Home of Golf*, J. & J. James Ltd., p. 1.

(2) cf article in *Golf Digest* for April, 1971, p. 59.

(3) Scott (ed): *Secrets of the Golfing Greats*, A. S. Barnes, 1965, p. 101.

(4) cf *Golf Digest*, November, 1971, p. 58.

(5) cf NIEPORTE and SAUER: *Mind Over Golf*, Doubleday & Co., Inc., 1968, p. 6.

(6) cf PALMER: *Situation Golf*, Saturday Review Press, 1972, p. 3.

# 2

# It Takes Time And Effort

*Most great golfers have paid a real price in time and effort for their achievements.*

Rufus Jones was a great Quaker philosopher. In one of his many publications he wrote, "One can always tell whether he is winning excellence by the ease with which he performs his tasks or his duties. The ease of excellence is, however, bought at a great price. It has cost labor and toil. It is the fruit of concentration and persistent effort."[1] Rufus Jones wasn't writing about golf. Indeed, we do not know that he even played the game. What he said, however, can be applied directly to golf and its mastery.

There is no real accomplishment without great effort. There is no significant accomplishment that is attained in a hurry. All success, all accomplishment takes time and energy, lots of energy. Those who have excelled in their chosen fields have usually been willing to spend extra time and effort. This is true in all areas of experience. Whether it is art, science, religion, or athletics it is those who have paid the price who have achieved.

**The Hogan Swing—a result of years of study and effort**

When Paderewski, the great pianist, was complimented for his mastery of the keyboard, he replied, "Before I was a master I was a slave."

Once in awhile there is someone with such natural ability, such an abundance of talent, that he rises to the top without undue effort, but it is the exception. This is especially true in golf.

Ben Hogan was voted the outstanding golfer of the last fifty years. A brief glance at his record convinces one that he deserves such recognition. He won the Open four times, the PGA twice, the Masters twice, the Colonial National Invitation five times, as well as many other tournaments. In 1953, he won the Open, the Masters, and then capped it all off by winning the British Open at Carnoustie. He did not play in the PGA that year. Who knows, he might have won "the grand slam" in one year. Just as much as Paderewski was the master in his field, so Hogan can rightfully be called a "master" in his.

He paid a great price for such a position. Probably no one ever spent more time and effort over a longer peiod of time than he. Success came late to Hogan. Sarazen and Ouimet won the Open at 20; Jones at 21; Hagen at 22; Nicklaus the first time he played it as a pro when he was only 22. Hogan turned pro at 19 but he was 36 before he won at Riviera in 1948. But he won.

It all began years earlier when he was working as a caddy at Glen Garden in Fort Worth. He said of those days, "I first met up with the game when I was twelve and I knew almost immediately that I wanted to make the game my life work."[2]

At first he played left handed, but, since few left handed clubs were available and since the only ones he could afford were used and cast off clubs, he learned to play right handed. "I must have been about thirteen when I started to work on my game conscientiously," he said. He's been working on it ever since.

The neighborhood where he lived had small lawns separated by hedges, a situation that still exists in Fort Worth. His own home was about six lawns from the grocery store. When he was sent to the store he never walked, he played his way. Letting each lawn become a practice green, he played over the hedges sometimes to the next lawn, sometimes two or three away; on occasion the whole distance. We don't know what the divots did to the lawns; we do know what it did for his golf game.

After he turned pro at nineteen his game needed lots of work and refinement. He was troubled with a bad hook with which he struggled for years. He observed the good players of his day and appropriated what he saw to his own game. He was a constant student of the game. Piece by piece he developed the concepts and the skill that resulted in his fantastically effective repeating swing. He observed, studied and practiced as no man had before him.

Grantland Rice, dean of American sportswriters and an avid golf fan, said, "It was evident sometime back that it was **not** genius but hard work that carried Ben to the top." Rice said that as a result of Hogan's exhaustive practice sessions he "hit fewer bad shots over a period of years than any other golfer."[3] Hogan lived by the philosophy that it is hard work that produces results. It is the price one pays for excellence.

Gary Player is another who spent inordinate amounts of time and effort in the development of his game. When he was just a young player he said he knew if he was ever going to compete with other professionals, or as he put it "become a champion", he would have to work harder than anyone else because of his size and weight. Both were against him. After he won the Masters in 1974 for the second time, he said, among other things, "No one works as hard at golf as I do." We shall again discuss Player and his willingness to work hard and long in the chapter on practice.

What was true of Hogan and Player has been true to some degree of all great golfers. There have been some of considerable natural ability who did not attain as much as was expected of them. They did not put forth the effort. There have been men who have surpassed others who had greater ability primarily because they were willing to invest the time and energy.

Such a one was Henry Cotton of Great Britain. Scott and Cousins, in their book on *Golf Immortals,* said, "There never has been a more dedicated golfer than Cotton. His thirst for practice and his hunger for knowledge of the game which he was determined to master were the keys which opened the door to his success."

In 1928 he came to America to play in the Open. He finished eighth. He was impressed by the Americans and went back to England "determined to practice even harder." Every week, he hit thousands of golf balls. He spent so many hours putting that he said it was easier to stay bent than stand up straight. He devoted all his free time to practicing, frequently going without lunch. After dinner at home he would go out to the garage and bang balls into a net.

In 1934 he gained his reward when he won the British Open at St. George's with opening rounds of 67 and 65. Some consider him the greatest professional golfer England has produced since Vardon. It didn't come easy. [(4)]

Dick Schaap, who edited Frank Beard's account of the Pro tour, spoke of the effort Beard put into the game. He gave up other sports to concentrate on golf. "When Frank was a teenager in Louisville, he played in the snow, chasing a red ball through drifts and slush. Sometimes, as he tried to master the game, he played as many as seventy-two holes in a single day, from sunup until past sundown, till his hands were raw, punishing himself for each shot he failed to execute perfectly."(5)

Everyone can't work at it as hard as Hogan, Player, Cotton, and Beard. Everyone shouldn't. Not everyone can or should make it a life work. For most of the thousands who enjoy the game golf is a hobby, an enjoyable and in many ways a valuable form of recreation. In watching the "masters" one should appreciate not only the excellence of their shots, but the time and effort that made them possible. This realization should also help to apply reasonable expectations to one's own game.

Only each individual can say how important golf is to him. Real achievement, here as elsewhere, comes only with time and effort.

(1) Jones: *The Testimony of the Soul,* Macmillian, 1939, p. 182.

(2) Hogan: *The Modern Fundamentals of Golf,* A. S. Barnes & Co., 1957, p. 15.

(3) Rice: *The Tumult and the Shouting,* A. S. Barnes & Co., 1954, p. 298.

(4) *The Golf Immortals* by Tom Scott and Geoffrey Cousins, copyright 1969, Hart Publishing Co., Inc., N.Y.

(5) Schaap: *Pro: Frank Beard on the Golf Tour,* Bantam Books, 1970, p. ix.

# 3

# There's No Substitute For The Fundamentals

*Good golfers have almost always been good students of the game.*

One does not think of successful golfers necessarily as students, much less as scholars. Most of them have little interest in the classroom and it is not unfair to say they are seldom found in the library. The majority do not spend much time reading, even books on golf. Successful golfers, however, are usually students of the game. The dictionary defines a student as "an attentive and systematic observer." In this sense they are students, good students.

Byron Nelson , when he set out to improve his game, made a study of all the successful golfers of his day. Rather than selecting any one as a model, he analyzed them all: Harry Cooper, Horton Smith, Ky Lafoon, Denny Shute, Johnny Revolta, Paul Runyan, Gene Sarazen, Walter Hagen and Craig Wood. In a very real sense he was a "systematic observer," a true student. He tried to figure out what each swing had in common with the others, how he could adapt it to his own game

Hogan did essentially the same thing. At first he copied the better amateurs around Fort Worth. When he was still caddying at Glen Garden he noticed that the left knee of one of the better players broke in to the right and his own to the left. He practiced knee action on the lawn at home until he wore out the grass. When he began the tour he noticed how Johnny Revolta varied his waggle for all his shots. Hogan felt it explained his effectiveness around the green which requires so much variety. He adopted this procedure for himself. So he studied the game by studying the experts and applied what he saw in endless experimentation and practice.

Hogan and Nelson were as thorough in their investigation as any scholar working on a research project.

All the experts have a knowledge of the basic fundamentals. They know the fundamentals of the grip, the stance, the backswing, the downswing, the follow through. They know the principles of the plane and all the fundamentals that comprise a good golf swing. As Gary Player says, if a player is to be a good golfer, he must know exactly what he's doing and why.

In addition to the fundamentals the experts also are aware of an infinitesimal number of other matters that comprise the subleties and possibilities in this fantastically interesting and at times simple but complicated game. Middlecoff's book, *Master Guide to Golf,*(1) has more than 145 divisions. The index has more than 500 different entries, each one dealing with a different aspect of the game. Gary Player has a book of golf instructions entitled *124 Lessons with Gary Player.*(2) Each lesson deals with a different topic.

Not every golfer has written a book on the fundamentals (although at times it seems that they have) but all have a knowledge of the fundamentals, plus the rules, plus the use of each of the fourteen clubs, plus many more details.

When one speaks of the mental side of golf he usually has reference to such attitudes as confidence and concentration. These are extremely important, as everyone recognizes. It is often overlooked that there is a tremendous amount of knowledge, information, and factual data to know about the game of golf if one would play it well. Devotees of other sports would probably disagree, but we doubt if there is any sport about which so much can be learned.

Good golfers must know the fundamentals mentioned above. They also must know what is required to hit a ball low under the trees or high over the trees. They must know how to read the slope of the green and estimate distance on the fairway. They must know how to hit the ball if it sits up on the grass, or is nestled into the grass, if it is on a bare spot, in a divot, or on hard pan. They must know what to expect if the ball is above their feet, below their feet, if the fairway slants uphill, or slopes downhill. They must know how weather conditions affect the flight of a ball, and how they must alter their play if it is cold or hot, windy or still, wet or dry.

They must know all about sand shots. They must know what to do if the sand is wet and packed, or fluffy and dry. They must alter their methods if the ball is buried in the sand, sitting on top of the sand, or settled into a footprint. They must know how to read the break of the green, how a ball rolls on different kinds of grass, how greens should be putted early in the morning and late in the afternoon after a day's wind has blown across them. This could be extended indefinitely. Suffice it to say, the good golfers have amassed an amazing amount of information and knowledge about the game and have stored it in their memory for use on the course. They not only know the game—they know the game in detail.

Attention to detail is always a mark of the artist. There is an old story (probably apocryphal) that when Michelangelo was working on his statue of David a friend visited him and asked what he had done since his last visit. Michelangelo is reported to have said he had touched up a feature, here; he had polished a portion there. The friend replied, "But these are only trifles." The artist's response was. "Trifles make perfection and perfection is no trifle."

The artists on the golf course paid attention to what others might call "trifles". The great Harry Vardon not only advised that one should keep his eye on the ball, but on the back of the ball. Gary Player, in studying a green, not only studies the slope of the green but how the cup is cut into the dirt. Ben Hogan knows how the ball comes out of grass or grass with clover in it. When they chip a shot to the green they note the break of the green, the lie of the ball, the grain of the grass around the ball, the possible effect of the wind—all this before making the shot.

The pros must consider every detail, even the temperature or their own adrenalin. Not to do so may cost them a lot of money. George Archer was playing the final round of the U.S. Open in 1972. He was contesting for the lead when he came to a short par three hole which he had birdied twice before. He figured it for an easy 9 iron which he had used so successfully twice previously. He hit what appeared to be a beautiful shot, except for one thing. It was way too long. It hit on the back of the green and bounced into a sand trap. He blasted out, took a bogey and dropped out of contention. He felt the reason it went so much farther than the day before was that he hadn't taken into account the temperature. It was a very warm day and golf balls travel farther when they are hot. It may have been the extra adrenalin that was the result of being charged up because he was in contention. We tend to hit the ball farther when we are excited. Perhaps it was both; at any rate it was a detail that made the difference.

One of these details may only come up once in a round, or even once in several rounds, but when it does come up, it can make a difference of one or two strokes. When we consider that when a man wins a four-day tournament by one stroke he is only one-quarter of a stroke better per day than his opponent who comes in second, we can understand the attention that must be given to detail.

They not only studied the details, they applied this knowledge to their own game. They studied their games in detail. Hogan tells how his game improved when he slightly modified the position of his thumb on the shaft. Nelson said concentrating on keeping the back of his left hand square to the target greatly increased his consistency. Palmer said that teeing the ball a fraction of an inch higher greatly improved his driving. We have heard that one of the leading pros tilts his tee slightly forward to remove all the resistance possible from the edge of the tee. Whether this is true or apocryphal, we do not know, but we do know that the details they know and apply are fantastic.

It might seem that so many details could be more confusing than helpful, but Frank Beard points out that a knowledge of the details involved eliminates rather than creates confusion.(3) Doug Ford says that one can only play good golf when he devotes "infinite attention" to many details.

Billy Casper, with the editors of *Golf Digest,* prepared a series of articles entitled "Billy Casper's Short Shot Almanac". He discussed in infinite detail the variety of shots that can be required around the green; for example, he described fourteen different kinds of shots from the sand. He included not only the regular shots, with the ball buried, the ball on a mound of sand, but also such situations as the ball being under the front lip, the ball in the sand but the feet out, etc. He said that one reason he is regarded as a good short game player is that he knows practically every way there is to play every possible short shot.

Since most shots can be played many ways he always chooses the simplest shot possible for any given situation. This allows for the greatest margin of error. Since he knows all the possibilities and also knows he has selected the simplest procedure possible he can play the shot with confidence. The result is a high rate of success.

His discussion of the short game applies to all the rest of one's game. A knowledge of details leads to confidence; confidence produces results.

Paul Harney who has been successful both as a touring pro and a teaching pro says the difference between the pro and the amateur is that the latter bets with hope but the pro bets with knowledge. There is no reason why an amateur can't have knowledge too if he will read, study and observe.

(1) cf Middlecoff: *Master Guide to Golf,* Prentice Hall, Inc., 1960.

(2) Player: *124 Lessons with Gary Player,* Follett Publishing Co., 1967.

(3) cf Beard: *Saving Strokes with Frank Beard,* Grossett and Dunlap, 1968, p. 34.

# 4

# Patience, Patience, Patience

*A good golfer needs a good swing—he also needs patience.*

The story is told of an oriental monarch who was asked the secret of his great serenity. He took a piece of paper and on it he wrote the word "patience" three times. This ancient monarch's secret is also one of the secrets of winning golf. Patience, patience, patience.

Someone has said, "The history of all achievement is largely the history of the achievement of patience." A study of biography will bear this out. The great artists, the great statesmen, the great scholars, the great scientists all achieved their eminence through both skill and patience.

Harry Emerson Fosdick, the great preacher, in a sermon on the theme of patience said, "Great things come slowly but they last." This is certainly true of golf. No one ever became a good golfer in a hurry. Take, for example, two of the greatest, Byron Nelson and Ben Hogan. Both waited a long time for real achievement. Hogan turned pro when he was nineteen but he was thirty-six before he won the Open at Riviera and started his great winning career.

Even Bobby Jones whose fantastic career as an amateur

probably never will be equaled did not have instant success. It's true he qualified for his first Open when he was only fourteen but it was some time before he won anything. In the seven years from 1916 to 1922, he played in eleven national championships but didn't win one. He was known as the golfer with the flawless swing who couldn't win. He credits his success to the achievement of patience. In fact, he contends that one not only needs patience in a career but in a tournament or a single round.

**The Incomparable Bobby Jones**

In the three years from 1923 to 1926 he played in ten championships and won five. He was second three times. In the seven years from 1923 to 1930 he won thirteen national titles and then retired at 28.

How does one account for such a change? Jones himself said it was a change in his attitudes, not an improvement in his shot-making. Most authorities would agree. The experts said he was as good mechanically at 19 as he ever was later. His attitudes, however, were drastically different. It wasn't a sudden or dramatic change. Very few people ever have achieved patience suddenly. "Great things come slowly but they last." It first came to fruitation in the National Open of 1923. He hadn't been playing well; his confidence was anything but strong. He saw others, particularly Bobby Cruickshank and Jack Hutchinson who had early leads, lose some of their advantage. He managed to hang on and win in a playoff.

He explained his change of attitude in an article with O. B. Keeler in these words, "So I suppose I began to understand that the other fellows all had their troubles, too; that I didn't have to go out and shoot four perfect rounds to win a major

Open championship, or even one perfect round, if I could just keep four decent rounds sticking together. I suppose I began instinctively to understand that one lost stroke didn't necessarily have to be redeemed at once; perhaps the other fellows were losing a stroke too."

As with all personality change, it wasn't complete and there were occasional set-backs. By the time of the National Amateur the next year the new pattern was pretty well established. He was engaged in a play-off and was two strokes down. "But I had a different attitude. Some way, I wasn't in that frantic hurry about getting those strokes back. It was as if something deep in my consciousness kept counseling patience. Patience."

Then he continued, "So maybe that is the answer—the stolid and negative and altogether unromantic attitude of patience. It is nothing new or original to say that golf is played one stroke at a time. But it took me many years to realize it. And it is easy to forget now. And it won't do to forget it in tournament golf."

He cited several of his tournament victories and credited most of them to patience and the ability it gave him to keep on hitting the ball. He repeated, "Maybe that is the answer—patience. Whatever I possess of it now must have been cultivated as I assuredly did not have it at first."(1)

He often said Old Man Par was the real opponent, but that Old Man Par is a "patient soul" and, "if you would travel the long route with him, you must be patient too."

It was almost forty years after his own victories, when people were asking him about the Masters, a tournament which his name made prestigious, that he said that the best advice he could give a man who wanted to win at Augusta was to be patient. We think Bobby Jones would agree that what is true at Augusta is true on every course where the game is played.

(1) Wind (ed): *The Complete Golfer,* article "The Immortal Bobby" by Bernard Darwin, Simon and Schuster, 1954, p. 279.

# 5

# Too Many Thoughts Spoil The Swing

*The experts all agree that you can have only one thought, or at most two thoughts, in mind when swinging a golf club.*

There is an old jingle which reads—

The centipede was happy quite
until a frog in fun
said, Pray which leg comes after which?
This left his mind in such a pitch
he lay distracted in the ditch
considering how to run.

There are an infinite number of things that influence and affect the golf swing. The grip, the stance, the distribution of weight, the straight left arm, etc., etc., etc.; they all are important. If one is going to play well, the more of these details he knows the better, but he better not be thinking of them while he swings. On this there is almost universal agreement.

You cannot think of a multitude of things, or even of three or four, in the brief time it takes to swing a golf club. It takes about one second to swing a golf club and one can't think of many details in that length of time. The results are bound to be disastrous if one tries. One would be in the same position as an expert typist if she tried to consider which finger to use next. She does it automatically.

Ernest Jones, whom some consider one of the greatest of all teaching pros, called it "paralysis by analysis". In his widely used book *Swing the Club Head* he pointed out that if a golfer tries to remember all the instruction he has received or read—wrists cocked, straight left arm, chin pointed, shoulder turned, hip shifted, leg braced, knee flexed, heel raised—while he is making his swing he will be lucky if he gets the club back at all. He says one should have but one thought in mind and that is "swing the clubhead."(1)

One can think of all the fundamentals on the practice tee. That is where they should be thought about and practiced until they are automatic—but not during the swing. Boros says that one must think of the wind, lie, traps, etc., but not while addressing the ball. Dave Hill says "one thought per swing is all I attempt."

A few years ago a young pro moved from the amateur ranks and immediately established himself as a coming star. He won a couple of events, finished high in some others and seemed well on his way. Then he faded just as rapidly and soon was having difficulty making the cut. Another professional who knew him and knew his game said that his chief problem was that "every time he drew the club back he had sixteen theories going through his mind". He was trying to think of too many things and it affected the smoothness as well as the effectiveness of his swing.

Most pros accept the idea that one can think of one or maybe two things during a swing to good advantage. Hogan says, "On the downswing you want to think of only one thing: hitting the ball." Tommy Armour says, "Get your club back any smooth way you can and then think of only one thing specifically: hitting the ball away with your hands."(2) Johnny Farrel thought only of his feet and getting a smooth pivot. Byron Nelson tried to see the clubhead flatten out the ball at impact. Billy Casper concentrates on taking the club back smoothly on the inside and hitting through the ball inside out.

Some suggest that the thing one thinks about should vary from day to day or week to week. Middlecoff advocates selecting one thing at the beginning of a round, maybe taking the club head back slowly, or keeping the head still. It may vary from day to day, but he selects one thing, and only one, and keeps that in mind that day. Gary Player once said he keeps two things in mind. He always concentrates on getting his weight to the left side and the second matter varies from day to day.

John Jacobs, teaching pro and coach of the British Walker cup team, says one of the best ways to develop a repetitive swing is to follow a "repetitive thought pattern". He contends that every golfer should have what he calls a "swing thought" that he uses each round. This key thought will vary from time to time depending on the golfer's game and the thing that needs attention. It should be just one thought at a time and should be decided upon during the pre round warm-up session.

He says that every good golfer he has known follows this practice either unconsciously or by plan. He tells the story of a well-known Irish amateur who would write such ideas as "Turn you fool" on his golf glove where he would be sure to see them at address.[3]

After Johnny Miller started the 1974 season by winning the first three tournaments of the year he was sought for many interviews and was the subject of many articles. He described a unique method to provide key thoughts while he was on the golf course. He keeps a list of key ideas on the back of an envelope. Sometimes he asks his caddy to write down a key idea on the envelope which he (the caddy) carries in his pocket.

The kinds of statements he writes on the envelope are simple and brief, such as "accelerate the whole club", "picture the swing", "don't rush it". Miller says that consulting the envelope to give him key thoughts is more effective than practice.

Some of the leading pros go one step farther than just having one thought in mind when making the golf swing. They insist that they think of "nothing" during the golf swing.

Some call it turning the swing over to the "subconscious", others call it leaving it to "muscle memory", or letting the muscles do the work. Some call it the "blank mind" theory. Basically they all mean the same thing. They contend that a player should not think of anything during the golf swing.

Tom Weiskopf, who had such a fantastic year in 1973 culminating in winning his first major championship at Troon in the British Open, says he tries to think only of the tempo of his swing. Dow Finsterwald, who was noted for his consistency, was asked what he tried to think of during the backswing and he replied that he simply tried to be as automatic as possible.

According to Ernest Jones this is exactly the way a person should play. He compared the golf swing to writing one's name. He pointed out that you don't need to give any thought to signing your name. You do it automatically and each signature is essentially the same as every other one, because you do it smoothly and automatically. If you try to think about it or copy it, however, then something else is introduced. The signature done freely and automatically will be the smoothest one. This, he says, is the way one should swing a golf club, smoothly, easily, and automatically.[(4)]

This is one of the chief purposes of practice, to get the feel of the swing so that one can play virtually without thinking about it—just swing the clubhead as Jones would say.

Sam Snead advocates a partial or modified approach. He calls "thinking" instead of "acting" the number one golf disease. He says that what he tries to do is just put his mind at rest by not thinking of anything in particular unless it is just a combination of all the good drives he's ever made. He tries to avoid thinking about such things as the crowd, or the match, or anything else that might distract. He calls it the trick of not thinking at all. He said if he did permit one key thought it would be simply "low and slow."(6)

Whether one accepts the "blank mind theory" or selects one thought doesn't seem to matter. The important thing is that one thought is the limit—then one does the rest automatically.

(1) Jones: *Swing the Clubhead,* Dodd Mead and Company, 1952, p. 97.

(2) Armour: *A Round of Golf With Tommy Armour,* Simon and Schuster, 1959, p. 20.

(3) cf Jacobs: *Practical Golf,* Quadrangle Books, 1972, pp. 138, 193.

(4) Jones, Ibid, p. 103.

(5) cf Snead: *Education of a Golfer,* quoted in *Golf and Club,* July, 1970, p. 38.

# 6

# Pace Reduces Pressure

*The successful golfers say, when the pressure increases, slow down the pace.*

Gary Player, in his book entitled *Positive Golf*, speaks of the importance of rhythm, timing and pace. He says Sam Snead is the best example of rhythm, Ben Hogan has the best timing, and Julius Boros is the classic illustration of pace.

Speaking of Boros, Player says, "He is always calm, never flustered. Before the day's play begins, whether it is the last round of the U.S. Open or a routine practice round, Boros takes it easy. He dresses leisurely, and leisurely moves to the practice tee, warms up leisurely, and leisurely moves to the first tee. Between shots he gives the appearance of being out for a pleasant walk. If he has to wait for the group ahead to clear the green, he shows not the least sign of impatience. If he hits a shot that doesn't satisfy him, he seems to shut it out of his mind completely."(1)

It doesn't mean there is no tension. Of course there is. Boros says it is present though it may not show. The "leisurely" approach mentioned above doesn't mean there is no desire to win. That is present, too, as Boros' record testifies. It does mean he has developed the capacity to control the pressure. He has found that pace, or the so-called leisurely approach to the game, produces winning results more often than any other.

Speaking of playing under pressure, Boros says the only thing he tries to do is to slow everything down. "Whenever I am in contention for a championship, and play has reached the fourth and deciding round, I deliberately try to slow down my game. The one thing I want to avoid is a too-fast, jerky and anxious swing." He says the thing he does not want to do is get too eager and hurry the shot. To watch Boros in a tournament is deceptive. He seems to be playing fast, at times almost carelessly. Nothing could be further from the truth. He says, "I do not waste time in swinging, but my actual swing is deliberate. This keeps me relaxed and helps me score the same or better as I have done earlier in the tournament before the pressure got so strong."(2)

Most successful golfers when they begin to feel pressure "slow everything down." Bobby Locke, four times winner of the British Open, deliberately conditioned himself to play slowly. Gary Player, who played often with Locke, said if Bobby Locke was dying of thirst he would reach out slowly for a glass of water. He also said that because he would do nothing in a hurry was one reason for Locke's success. This is what Sam Snead means when he says to himself, "Draw the bead easy, boy, or there won't be a turkey dinner tonight."

Bruce Crampton was interviewed on television early in the 1974 season. He hadn't been winning as he had in 1973 when he started out so well. He explained it this way, "A lot of times there's just not enough minutes to do everything, play golf, attend to business, travel. I suddenly found myself driving fast, eating fast, walking fast and consequently I began swinging the club too fast. Finally I just had to slow down everything. And I'm playing better. In fact I'm on the edge of playing super again. You've got to maintain an even tempo on the tour. Pacing is the answer."

Bruce Devlin, in a chapter he included in his book on

**The experts say, "Slow down the pace", but Chuck Courtney and Tommy Aaron didn't seem to hear**

playing in tournaments, said that one of the main things to remember in playing in competition is the importance of the tempo at which one plays. He said, "By this I mean the pace at which you move around the course." He said one of the first things he had to learn when he began competing on the American tour was to slow everything down. He had played very fast as an amateur in Australia but he found this wouldn't work under the added pressure. "I have learned to slow down when tension builds up," he said, "Don't rush the vital shots. Take extra warm up swings, and accept the challenge without hedging."(3)

Gary Player takes this matter of pace so seriously that he begins to set his pace not only before he gets to the course but several days before a tournament begins. When he won the U.S. Open at St. Louis he said, "I practiced pace for a whole week before the opening round on Thursday, and between rounds. I deliberately did things more slowly than my nature normally dictates. When I spoke to people, I spoke slowly. I set a calm, slow pace for myself in all things—eating, dressing, going to and from the course."(4) While many things went into winning the tournament, there is no doubt in Player's mind that pace was one of them.

If one were to trace the emphasis on pace or tempo to one thing or one event it would probably be Harry Vardon's visit to the United States in 1900. He had already won the British

Open three times and during his tour added the U.S. Open to his titles. He toured the country playing exhibition matches and giving demonstrations. People were impressed by the "lazy perfection" of his swing. Everyone knows that his grip became standard for the majority of golfers. It was not only the grip that was copied. Scott and Cousins say, "American golfers took the Vardon grip, the Vardon swing, the Vardon passion for accuracy and the Vardon imperturbability as their models."(5)

Another Britisher, Tony Jacklin, was in contention for the U.S. Open in 1970. He finished the third round with a five-stroke lead. When he arrived for the final round he found a one word sign taped on his locker by two of his golf professional friends. It was the word "tempo". Apparently it worked for he withstood all pressures and won by seven strokes to be the first Britisher to win the U.S. Open in more than twenty years.

(1) Player: *Positive Golf,* McGraw Hill, 1968, p. 80, 81.

(2) Boros: *How to Play Golf With An Effortless Swing,* Prentice Hall, Inc., 1964, p. 28.

(3) Devlin: *Play Like the Devil,* Doubleday & Co., 1970, p. 143.

(4) Player: Ibid., p. 82.

(5) *The Golf Immortals* by Tom Scott and Geoffrey Cousins, copyright 1969, Hart Publishing Co., Inc., N.Y.

# 7

# Relaxation Can Be Learned

*The good golfers agree relaxation is necessary for a smooth swing.*

Dai Rees, noted British player, says the cure for most mis-hit shots is "to make sure your swing is smooth and relaxed." Gary Player, speaking of competition says, "At all times one should be relaxed, both in mind and body." David Thomas, speaking of bunker play said, "I will tell you first of all the secret of getting well out of a bunker. It is to relax."(1) Such statements are common among winning golfers.

Relaxation is necessary in all sports. On a Monday evening in April 1974, Henry Aaron broke Babe Ruth's all time home run record when he hit his 715th home run into the left field bull pen in Atlanta. Many baseball authorities credit much of Aaron's success to his ability to be relaxed at the plate. In fact it has been said of Aaron that he is the only player that takes a nap between pitches. This does not mean he is careless or inattentive. At least his opposing pitchers don't think so. It doesn't mean there is no tension or pressure. One can hardly imagine the pressure he must have felt as he was approaching 714 and 715. Even so he managed to control the tension and reduce the pressure. Undoubtedly much of this was due to his capacity to remain relaxed in the pressure of a tense situation.

What is true of Aaron to a phenomenal degree is true of all athletes to some degree, especially golfers. This can be seen at almost any tournament. During the practice rounds a player may shoot a very fine score. He is in the low 70's or even the high 60's. He's playing relaxed. As soon as the regular rounds begin, however, it is a different story. What has happened? It is the same course. The pin placements may be a bit tougher, but there isn't that much difference. The pressure of the tournament, the desire to do well, the presence of a gallery have all increased the tension and destroyed his relaxation. As a result his swing is not quite so smooth.

Dr. Richard C. Procter, the chairman of the Department of Psychiatry at the Bowman Gray School of Medicine, Wake Forest University, wrote an article in the 1974 *PGA Book of Golf.* He contrasted the mental attitudes necessary for good golf with the mental attitudes that prove effective in other sports especially contact sports such as football, basketball or boxing. He referred to a term frequently heard in all sports—being "psyched up".

"Being psyched up", he says, "is fine for football players, basketball players, boxers and track stars. The adrenalin starts flowing, the heart rate increases, the blood pressure increases and the respiratory rate increases, forcing more oxygen into the blood stream. That's fine if you're a football player and you're going to overpower your opponent. In golf, however, it's just the reverse. You've got to be relaxed, in complete control of yourself and your emotions. You can't be psyched up and be relaxed at the same time and in golf it's the one with the relaxed swing who is going to have more success."(3)

Some pressure, some tension is inevitable. Some feeling of tension is good. If one feels no tension at all he would have no incentive, there would be no challenge. It would take the fun out of the game. There is no danger of feeling too relaxed, at least not for most of us. John Jacobs, well-known teaching pro in England, says the good golfers are all "sensibly perturbed". They are aware of the situation; they feel the tension, but they are able to remain relaxed and maintain their poise.[4]

Arnold Palmer relates relaxation and concentration. "The mental approach that golf requires," he says, "is a peculiar and complicated mixture of abiding confidence and patient resignation, of intense concentration and total relaxation." This he says reduces tension. "I've got to concentrate the way a golfer is meant to concentrate, in that relaxed, free and easy way that will let the swing flow."[5]

Tom Nieporte equals relaxation with confidence. Like so many others he stresses the importance of the ability to relax. He also emphasizes the need for confidence. The two he says are almost synonymous. The man who is confident can play relaxed. The man who can stay relaxed remains confident.[6]

What these men are saying is in accord with good learning theory. Physiologists like Edmund Jacobsen and psychotherapists like Josef Wolpe have known this for a long time. They have demonstrated it in their laboratories and observed it with their patients. There are several simple statements that summarize their findings:

(1) All behavior is learned. This is basic. Tension is one form of behavior. Therefore all tension is learned. It is learned by thousands of daily repetitions.
(2) The opposite of tension is relaxation. You can't be tense and relaxed at the same time.
(3) Relaxation is also a form of behavior. Therefore relaxation can also be learned.
(4) By learning or cultivating the capacity to relax one reduces tension.

This applies to golf in that the less tension the better the coordination. The more one can relax, the more he reduces tension. The more he improves his coordination, the more effectively he plays. This is what Palmer means when he says he must concentrate "in that relaxed, free and easy way that will let the swing flow".

Bruce Devlin says this is true of all aspects of the game but especially of putting. He points out that whatever grip or putting stance is used, good golfers never putt with the body tensed. When the body is tense it reduces feel or touch. When the body is relaxed it increases the touch one has with the putter.(6)

The important thing about all this is that relaxation can be learned. Psychotherapists are teaching people to relax all the time. Dr. Jacobsen, referred to above, wrote a book about it entitled *You Must Relax.*(7) He was talking about patients who needed to reduce anxiety and check some physical symptoms. His is a rather elaborate system of learning to relax one set of muscles at a time. Others simply request that the person spend fifteen minutes a day and concentrate on the muscles of the body, moving progressively from the head to the toes, slowly relaxing each set of muscles as one goes. This done over a period of time replaces the habit of tension with one of relaxation, then one applies it in more active situations.

We repeat: relaxation reduces tension–relaxation can be learned.

(1) These quotes all were taken from Scott: *Secrets of the Golfing Greats,* A. S. Barnes, Co., 1965, p. 132, 45, 112.

(2) Proctor, article in *1974 PGA Book of Golf,* Professional Golfer's Association of America, p. 30.

(3) cf Jacobs: *Practical Golf,* Quadrangle Books, 1972, p. 145.

(4) Palmer: *My Game and Yours,* Simon & Schuster, 1963, p. 61, 70.

(5) cf Nieporte and Sauer: *Mind Over Golf,* Doubleday, Co., 1968, p. 13.

(6) cf Devlin: *Play Like the Devil,* Doubleday, Co., 1970, p. 110.

(7) Jacobsen: *You Must Relax,* McGraw-Hill, 1957.

# 8

# Tension Reducing Techniques

*Almost anything that reduces tension improves the golf swing.*

We live in a time that has been called the age of anxiety. Tension is a characteristic of our culture. Golf can help reduce the tension of our lives, or in some cases it can increase it. One thing is certain: Tension is the great enemy of the golf swing. All the experts agree on this. Anything that reduces tension is an aid to the golf swing. They agree on this also.

In the last chapter we discussed relaxation training as one means of reducing tension. There are many other methods that have been tried and found useful.

Most of the pros have discussed or developed their own means of reducing tension. Sam Snead talks to the ball. He says he believes in giving the ball some "sweet talk" on the tee. "This isn't going to hurt a bit," he will say, or, "Sambo is just going to give you a nice little ride." He says that by talking to the ball, acting as if it is human, he distracts himself and leaves no time for "thoughts of this and that".[1]

Lee Trevino reduces tension by bantering with the crowd. The crowd loves it and he keeps free from tension as well.

Gary Player can be seen bending over and exhaling deeply before a shot. Bobby Nichols also takes a deep breath and lets it out slowly before addressing the ball. Basketball players often use this technique before shooting free throws. The deep breathing helps to control tension.

When Dutch Harrison was playing the tour he refused to think or discuss golf between rounds. He played his practice rounds casually. During actual play he kept his fingers extended as he walked down the fairway. If one doubles his hand into a fist, Harrison said, it creates tension in the arms. By extending the fingers he reduced tension physically and mentally as well.

Tommy Bolt describes tension in his own unique way. He says, "Every club you pull out of the sack feels like the bag strap in your hands. It's wiggly like a snake. You can't take the stick away from the ball. It is the most helpless feeling in the world."(2) He feels the best solution for such a situation is prevention. He looks with some skepticism on the various remedies he has heard. One suggestion is to close your eyes and breathe deeply ten times. Bolt's comment was that after the ten count you've got to open your eyes and you've got the same shot staring you in the face. He feels the best tension reducing influence is a combination of concentration and confidence.

Bobby Nichols reduces tension by reminding himself of the basic fundamentals. In the 1970 Dow Jones, which had the largest cash prize ever offered, $60,000.00, he had a fourteen foot putt on the 18th green. If he made it he won, if not he went into a play off.

It was described as the richest putt in history—$4,285.00 a foot. He was well aware how tension could spoil his concentration and could cause him to jerk the stroke. He knew full well if he looked up too soon to see how the ball was rolling it could affect his shot. He said on such occasions he recalls the basic fundamentals of a good stroke. Describing the incident these were his words, "I said 'Keep your head steady, Bobby, and hit that ball as solidly as possible.'" The ball rolled up to the cup, hesitated a moment and dropped in.(3)

Jack Burke, Jr., says the advice given elsewhere in this study–to play one shot at a time–reduces tension. He says he has seen many club players spoil a round by thinking of the results of the round instead of the immediate shot. "They think about the trophy and getting their names in the paper and they forget about hitting the ball properly." All such ideas increase tension. Hubert Green, one of the promising young stars on the tour, has demonstrated an unusual capacity to play well under pressure. He said basically the same thing Burke said, "I've always believed that one shot is independent of another." This helps him keep cool.

Bruce Devlin points out that if one is to do well in competition he must develop interests away from the course that are relaxing (which reduces tension) and enable him to "let off steam." Billy Casper, Julius Boros, and Jack Nicklaus are ardent fishermen. Gary Player likes to dance. Devlin himself likes horse racing. Gene Littler collects and reworks old cars. He possesses three old Rolls Royces, a 1914 Model T roadster, and a 1963 Jaguar. His wife drives a 1939 Rolls Royce to the market, while he drives a 1929 Ascot Phaeton. Recently the entire family drove a 1924 Rolls Roadster a distance of 90 miles to Disneyland. He loves to tinker, polish and work with these old cars. He says when he's working on his cars he forgets all about the three-putt greens.

This is more of a problem for the touring pro who plays pressure golf all the time than it is for the amateur. However, Gene Sarazen says it is good advice for the amateur golfer who wants to play well. He points out that anyone can go stale if he plays too much and this can affect his whole game causing both mental and physical errors. In a book written primarily for the senior golfer entitled, *Better Golf After Forty,* he doesn't recommend that a person play golf every day even when it's possible. If a person will go fishing, boating, or do something different he is not as likely to get tired of golf and actually may improve his game. He said what he did when he got tired of tournaments was to put his clubs away and go to his farm. Pretty soon he found he wanted to get them out and was ready to play again.[5]

Anything, in or off the course, that reduces tension will improve one's golf and have other beneficial effects as well.

(1) Snead: *Education of a Golfer*, Crest Books, 1962, p. 66.

(2) *The Hole Truth* by Tommy Bolt with Jimmy Mann. Copyright 1971 by Tommy Bolt. Reprinted by permission of J. B. Lippincott Company.

(3) cf *Golf Digest,* November, 1970, p. 19.

(4) cf *Golf Magazine,* March, 1971, p. 75.

(5) cf Sarazen: *Better Golf After Forty,* Harper & Row, 1967, p. 119.

Gary Player has learned to be relaxed under tension

# 9

# Imagination And Visualization

*The good golfers use imagination and visualization to help them play well.*

William James, the great psychologist, once said if there is a contest between the imagination and the will, the imagination will win every time. Every psychologist knows that the power of suggestion can be exceedingly strong. Most professional golfers have not read William James' *Principles of Psychology* but they utilize this principle all the time. Byron Nelson says, "Imagine exactly where you want the shot to finish." Tom Weiskopf said in an interview, "Disciplined imagination is the essence of championship golf." Horton Smith, in an article "Using Your Imagination in Your Golf Game," pointed out that this is a part of the touring pros' ability which cannot be observed by the gallery, but it is there. He also said it is a phase of golf that anyone–pro or amateur–can develop.(1)

Walter Hagen advocated the use of the imagination years ago. He was speaking of trouble shots, but he went on to include all shots. "Trouble shots are surprisingly easy if you activate your imagination. You simply must be able to imagine exactly what flight the ball will take before you can play any shot well."[2]

Ernest Jones, one of the most successful of teachers, says this is the way to improve one's swing. "There is only one way to become a good golfer," he says, "By carrying a clear mental picture of the swing as being one movement you will insure the coordination of all the members of the body. . ."

**Johnny Miller visualizes each shot before he hits**

Johnny Miller, after his dramatic win in the 1973 Open with a final round 63, said in an interview he did several things before each shot. First he checked the lie, the wind and the distance. Then he sets up and gets comfortable. Then he tells himself to take it back slow and keep his head still but the last thing he does is picture the swing he wants to make. Ben Hogan's concept of the plane has been one of the most influential. He describes it with ample illustrations in his book *The Modern Fundamentals of Golf.* He says, "Perhaps the best way to visualize what the plane is and how it influences the swing is to imagine that, as the player stands before the ball at address, his head sticks out through a hole in an immense pane of glass that rests on his shoulders as it inclines upward from the ball." The pane of glass sets the plane of the swing. If his hands rise up they break the glass and ruin the swing. If they drop too low it is equally unfortunate.[3]

The experts advise a golfer to use his imagination when he is playing, first to plan the shot, then to visualize it before he swings. Eddie Merrins, teaching pro at the Bel-Air Country Club in Los Angeles, wrote an article on the short game. He spoke of the stance, stroke, etc., but he also said, "You have to 'design' the shot in your mind that you think can best get you close to the hole. . ." His concluding statement was, "A good tip in playing pitch and chip shots is to paint a mental picture of the shot before the execution. Then, when you select the club, it's just a matter of positive execution of the picture you have in mind.(4)

Paul Hahn is best known as a trick shot artist, but he has also made a careful study of the game. "Good golfers," he says, "never think about how to hit the ball–they think about where to hit it. They have a picture in their minds of the ball in flight and the target."(5)

Many of the great golfers, such as Byron Nelson, Ben Hogan, Sam Snead, and Dave Marr, have made statements of how they utilized visualization before hitting a shot. Gary Player says, "I've conditioned myself, for instance, to visualize the path of my shots before I play them. . .I try to direct my thinking toward making a good shot. I visualize how a good shot will look and feel. Then I give it the best stroke or swing I have."(6)

Arnold Palmer in answering a question in *Golf Magazine's* "Champ's Clinic" said, "Try to feel comfortable over the ball at address and make sure you picture the flight of the ball mentally before you attempt to hit it. Then swing smoothly and don't try to force it."(7)

Tommy Bolt compares it to a motion picture show. He says you are supposed to see each shot just the way you want it to be played as if it were on a motion picture screen in your mind's eye. Then you simply carry it out with your actual swing.(8)

Jack Nicklaus in his new book *Golf My Way* also advocates the motion picture technique. He says he never hits a shot, even in practice, without having a clear picture of it just the way he wants it to be, in his head. First he sees a color movie of the ball where he wants it to end, then a scene with the ball in flight, then a scene which pictures the kind of a swing that will make it possible. He says he will not even select a club until he has seen this "Hollywood spectacular." But he warns that the movies should always picture a perfect shot.(9)

There is no place where this is more important than in putting. Here the golfers use both imagination and visualization. Many ideas are suggested. One is to visualize a line going from the ball to the hole. Some prefer to visualize a path, the width of the cup running back through the ball to the putter.

These ideas will be discussed in a later chapter on putting. The whole idea is to inspire confidence. Here, as always, the visualization should be positive. Gary Player says, "Try to get a mental picture of the ball following the correct line and traveling at the right speed to take it into the middle of the cup." Tommy Bolt says that on one of his real good days he can see those 20 footers roll into the cup before he ever bends over to stroke the ball.

The imagination is used in many other ways to aid in executing the right swing or to understand specific shots. Practically every book of golf instruction and every issue of a golf magazine has one or more illustrations of how someone has used the imagination to help get a picture of the shot. The concept of swinging in a barrel is one of the oldest and most familiar. The purpose, of course, is to reduce sway. Bob Toski, in a new book of golf instruction entitled *The Touch System for Better Golf,* makes many such suggestions, all with appropriate illustrations. To learn to accelerate the clubhead he suggests imagining a child on a swing. To be sure one is lined up properly he compares it to standing on a railroad track. The feet are on one rail, the ball on the other and the club at impact is going down that rail. To guarantee extending the clubhead low beyond the ball he visualizes an airplane taking off. To get the feel of the downswing he compares it to a canoe being gradually drawn toward a waterfall. The release is compared to the snap of a rubber band held between two fingers and released like a sling shot. The hands work together like a good dance team.(10)

Many suggestions have been made for helping with sand shots. The fried egg shot is the most familiar. The golfer is advised to imagine the ball is the yoke of a fried egg. If one just hits the whole egg out of the sand the shot will be about right. The dollar bill shot is the same idea. One imagines the ball is the portrait on the dollar bill and then hits the entire dollar bill out of the sand.

Jack Nicklaus says one should practice using his imagination as much as he practices making shots. "The practice tee," he says, "is the place to train yourself to picture the ball in flight, and its positive result, before you actually swing. The ability to use imagination is one of the most valuable assets a golfer can possess."(11)

(1) cf Wind: *The Complete Golfer,* Simon and Schuster, 1954, p. 297.

(2) Nieporte & Sauer: *Mind Over Golf,* Doubleday & Co., 1968, p. 67.

(3) Hogan: *Fundamentals of Golf,* A. S. Barnes Co., 1957, p. 77.

(4) *Golf and Club,* March 1971, p. 34, 5.

(5) *Golf Digest,* May 1970, p. 43.

(6) Player: *Positive Golf,* McGraw Hill, 1967, p. 87.

(7) *Golf Magazine,* September 1971, p. 11.

(8) *The Hole Truth* by Tommy Bolt with Jimmy Mann. Copyright 1971 by Tommy Bolt. Reprinted by permission of J. B. Lippincott Company.

(9) Nicklaus: *Golf My Way,* Simon & Schuster, 1974, p. 81.

(10) Toski: *The Touch System for Better Golf,* Simon & Schuster, 1971

(11) *Golf Digest,* April 1972.

# 10

# Positive And Negative Thinking

*All the experts agree that you have to think positively to play winning golf.*

One thing is definite in all the discussions about concentration, imagination, visualization, confidence, planning, strategy, whatever the topic—it all depends on positive or confident thinking. On this there is complete agreement. From Harry Vardon to Jack Nicklaus this is true. Arnold Palmer has said many times, "You shouldn't underestimate the power of a positive thought."

They all recognize the power of positive thinking. The corollary is also true but is not as frequently recognized. Negative thinking can be equally influential. Harry Vardon knew this a long time ago. He said, "At the beginning of a match do not worry yourself with the idea that the result is likely to be against you. By reflecting thus upon the possibilities of defeat one often becomes too anxious and loses one's freedom of style. . ." Again, he said, "At a crisis in a match, some golfers, fighting desperately for victory. . .give themselves up when on the tee to hideous thoughts of all the worst ways in which they have ever made that particular drive and of the terrible consequences that ensued. This is fatal. . .If he cannot school himself to think that he is going to make the best drive of his life, just when it is most wanted, he should not try to think of anything at all."(1)

Arnold Palmer, one of the best of the positive thinkers

In 1971 Billy Casper had what many termed a bad year. It is true that he earned almost $108,00.00, which most of us would consider pretty successful, but, comparatively speaking (and almost everything is comparative in golf), he didn't play as well as he usually does. He explained the reasons in a magazine article early the next year. As he looked back over the year, he said, "My real problem was lack of concentration, but I didn't realize that until later. Those double-bogey swings were not caused by faulty technique, although my technique certainly was very faulty at the moment I hit the ball miles right or left. The root cause was mental, not mechanical. Almost every double bogey I made in 1971 was born of indecision, which in turn was bred by lack of concentration. Through sheer weariness or sloppiness, every now and again I simply would not determine precisely enough what I needed to do before I actually tried to do it. On a drive I would not **positively** select a target area. On an approach shot I would not **positively** decide which club I needed. On an approach putt, I would not **positively** decide the amount of break or the speed of the green. The result too often was an indecisive stroke and double-bogey."(2)

There are many misconceptions about concentration in golf. The implication is that one must concentrate, that concentration in itself is good. Negative concentration can create more problems than it solves. Bobby Nichols tells what the "power of negative thinking" did to him in the 1964 World Series of Golf. He was playing the 16th hole of the Firestone Country Club. It was a long par five. He had a good drive and a good second shot. All he had left was a hundred yard approach shot over a pond to the green. He said to himself, "If I don't hit this shot just right, it could fall into the water." Splash! That is exactly what happened.

A few years ago when Palmer was at his best, a pro whom we will not name, admitted before a tournament that most of them had conceded the tournament to Palmer and were just playing for second place. Palmer and this pro came to the 72nd (last) hole even up. Palmer double-bogeyed it. The other pro triple bogeyed it. The power of negative thinking! He fulfilled his own prophecy.

The good golfers almost force themselves to think positively. They always have. When Walter Hagen was at his best he used to take his stance on the first tee, wink at the gallery and say, "I wonder who will be second in this one." There wasn't a doubt in his mind but what he could win. They say he was never short on putts because he expected to make them, and he knew if he missed he could make it coming back.

As much as any other aspect of the intangibles of golf, cultivating the capacity to think positively is one of the most important. Tommy Bolt said, you must not approach golf with a single negative thought. Arnold Palmer said in a recent publication, "Your performance has a way of living up to your expectations".(3)

Eddie Meriam, teaching pro at Bel-Air Country Club in Los Angeles, referring to trouble shots particularly, but also to any shot, says, "You must feel confident that you can pull the shot off or don't take it."(4) There might be occasions when if this advice were taken literally one would have to put his clubs back in the bag and go home. In the main, however, it is a position with which most pros would agree.

Jimmy Demaret emphasizes the same idea. "Don't play the shot you're not sure about." To state this positively: Do play the shot you are most sure about. Select the club you have the most confidence in. Make a decision and play the shot with confidence. Tom Nieporte says the same thing. "If there's any doubt in your mind that you can make a certain shot, chances are you won't make it. If you believe you can, chances are you will."(5)

Gary Player's formula for winning golf has three points. (1) You've got to want to win. (2) You've got to believe you can win. (3) You've got to think only positive thoughts. The title of the book in which these statements are found is appropriately enough *Positive Golf*.(6)

Tom Nieporte, in his study of the psychological factors influencing leading pros, frequently related it to the amateur. He stressed the fact that many golfers don't play up to their potentialities because they don't believe they can. It is his feeling, and one shared by most pros, that most golfers could improve vastly if they really wanted to and believed they could.

A golfer must know the fundamentals to be sure. He must concentrate. But, as Tom Nieporte says, "Your concentration should be entirely on the positive aspect of your shot." This is the power of positive thinking in golf. As Sam Snead says, "You've got to think like a winner to win."

(1) Scott: *Secrets of the Golfing Greats,* A. S. Barnes & Co., 1965, p. 150, 152.

(2) *Golf Digest,* April 1972, p. 4.

(3) Palmer: *Situation Golf,* Saturday Review Press, 1972, p. 181.

(4) *Golf & Club,* July 1970, p. 13.

(5) Nieporte & Sauer: *Mind Over Golf,* Doubleday, 1968, p. 12.

(6) cf Player: *Positive Golf,* McGraw Hill, 1967, p. 17.

(7) Nieporte, Ibid., p. 17.

# 11

# Concentration Is A Must

*Good golfers agree that you have to concentrate to play well.*

A long time ago the great Harry Vardon said, "In a majority of cases concentrated purpose is the secret of victory." Henry Cotton, his fellow countryman, said, "Concentration is the major facet in scoring well."(1)

Arnold Palmer said, "I have never known a great performer—and over the years I have known champions in many sports—who didn't have the ability to concentrate completely. What do I mean by concentration?" he asks, "I mean focusing totally on the business at hand and commanding your body to do exactly what you want it to do."(2)

Bobby Mitchell, who beat Jack Nicklaus in a playoff for the Tournament of Champions title, said it was due to his concentration. "That's one thing I've learned out here," he said, "You have to get yourself in a trance." In fact he was concentrating so well he was unaware that Nicklaus broke his driver on the 16th tee and finished without it.

Tommy Bolt said, "Once you've acquired a golf swing, then the rest of it depends on your ability to concentrate. After you have improved that swing, concentration is 75

**Bruce Crampton, a study in concentration**

percent of golf. That's the reason I refer to it so often. It's important because it is 75 percent of my trade."(3)

One of the most impressive things in watching a tournament is the obvious concentration of such players as Player, Palmer, Nicklaus, Crampton, etc., all the winners. They all demonstrated "concentrated purpose", especially if they were in contention. But none more than Hogan. Grantland Rice said of Hogan, "Concentration and determination—unbroken. That means Hogan."(4) He quoted Craig Wood who said that many men had great swings but "Hogan knows what he's doing all the time. He concentrates better than anyone I ever saw."

Many incidents have been repeated about Hogan's amazing powers of concentration. Hogan had breakfast with a friend the day of a tournament. All was friendly. Later the friend met him in the locker room. Hogan didn't even speak. Apparently he didn't even see him—he had already started his concentration. Sam Snead, who played with Hogan many

**No one concentrates better than Hogan**

times, said that when Hogan was at his best Hogan would wish him "good luck" on the first tee, then go into his isolation booth and not come out until the round was over. Jimmy Demaret, long time friend and competitor with Hogan, said it was untrue that Hogan wouldn't talk during a round. He said he spoke to him on every green. He'd say, "You're away."

Hogan himself said, "I know that I have sometimes concentrated so hard on the shot I was going to hit that I honestly felt the shot could not fail to come off exactly as I intended. On these occasions I had the definite sensation that I had really hit the shot before I even started my club back."(5)

There are different degrees and different expressions of concentration. Hogan and Player are examples of intense concentration. It is all-inclusive, all-consuming, seemingly continuous. When Player is in contention for a tournament he is the very picture of concentration. You can see it in his face and in his manner as he walks down the fairway, as he studies the situation and plans the shot.

Such concentration is not easy. Henry Cotton has pointed out that it takes a lot of energy to concentrate for an entire round. It is a lot of work. It can be very fatiguing. He said he was often in good enough physical condition to walk the distance without tiring at all, but the concentration was what was so demanding. Yet he pointed out that if you relax the concentration, even on a short putt, it can cost a stroke just as much as if you hit a bad drive.

Julius Boros, Lee Trevino, and Doug Sanders practice intermittent concentration. Trevino and Sanders banter with the gallery, talk to the caddy, the marshals, in Trevino's case, with anybody who will listen. Boros contends one shouldn't attempt to concentrate all the time. It creates too much tension. During the walk down the fairway he says he intentionally thinks of other things, the scenery, the clouds, etc. He saves his concentration until he approaches the ball. There is plenty of time to concentrate then. Trevino and Sanders kid and banter a lot but they concentrate when they are over the ball. All good golfers do.

Arnold Palmer favors what he calls relaxed concentration. "To me concentration means a total and forward-looking relationship between the mind and the challenge. The secret of that relationship is not tension but relaxation."[(6)]

When good golfers run into a few bad rounds they usually credit it to a loss of concentration. Frank Beard, leading money winner in 1969, explained a let-down. "I just haven't had my good concentration. . .I've been worrying about the holes I've already played and the holes I'm going to play, instead of concentrating on just one thing, the shot I'm about to hit."

Beard's statement points out the first of three important factors about concentration. It must be specific, it must be positive, and during the execution of the shot it must be uninterrupted.

The story is told of a woman who heard a lecture by

Edward Bok on how to use one's time. After the lecture she said, "Dr. Bok, I'm going to concentrate." He said, "Good, on what?" She said, "Oh, on lots of things."

When a golfer concentrates on "lots of things" the results are likely to be disastrous. It was said of Walter Hagen that he would not let himself think about the hole he had just played or the one that he was about to play. The only pin in the world for Hagen was the one he was shooting for at that moment."

Concentration must also be positive. We repeat–negative concentration produces results just as effectively as positive concentration. Billy Casper says there are two kinds of putters: those who worry about how to miss a putt, and those who concentrate on how to get it in the hole. What is true of putting is equally true of all the rest of the game.

Concentration, as much as possible, must also be uninterrupted, even though distractions occur. Jack Nicklaus is another who has mastered this aspect of the game as well as his long drives. In fact, he learned it very young. He describes an incident that occurred when he was still an amateur. He was playing in the World Amateur Team Championship when he was only twenty years old. He said his concentration was "astonishing". "I was crouching over the four footer I needed for my par on the eighteenth when a gust of wind blew my cap off. I hardly noticed it. I kept on working on the putt and holed it."(7)

All good golfers have developed their powers of concentration, or they wouldn't be good golfers. As Gary Player says, ". . .if you don't concentrate you're not playing your best golf."

(1) Scott: *Secrets of the Golfing Great,* A. S. Barnes, 1965, p. 144.

(2) Palmer: *Situation Golf,* Saturday Review Press, 1972, p. 4.

(3) *The Hole Truth* by Tommy Bolt with Jimmy Mann. Copyright 1971 by Tommy Bolt. Reprinted by permission of J. B. Lippincott Company.

(4) Rice: *The Tumult and the Shouting,* A. S. Barnes, 1954, p. 298.

(5) Hogan: *The Modern Fundamentals of Golf,* A. S. Barnes, 1957, p. 66.

(6) Palmer: *My Game and Yours,* Simon and Schuster, 1963, p. 64.

(7) Nicklaus: *The Greatest Game of All,* Simon and Schuster, 1965, p. 112.

# 12

# Confidence Is The Name Of The Game

*All the experts agree—confidence is the basic psychological necessity to playing winning golf.*

Of all the intangibles in golf, none is more important to possess, more elusive to attain, and more difficult to describe than confidence. No one knows for sure what it is, or why one man has it and another doesn't. No one knows why a person can have it one day and not the next. No one understands how it can be lost so quickly, or regained so unexpectedly. But of its value there can be no doubt. Bobby Jones once said, "Without confidence a golfer is little more than a hacker." Jack Nicklaus said, "There is no way you can overestimate the power of confidence or its results in golf."

A few years ago a young player who was new to the tour made some pretty optimistic, even cocky, statements about how many tournaments he expected to win and how much money he thought he would make. Many writers and players were critical of his brashness and apparent over confidence. Others, including Nicklaus, said his attitude wasn't all bad. He thought he could win and said so. As Nicklaus put it,

**Ben Hogan drives with confidence**

quoting an old adage, "If you don't have faith in yourself, nobody's going to have faith in you."

In any activity where competition is involved confidence is a key factor. Given two teams or two players of equal ability, the one who is the most confident will win every time. Bobby Nichols, who went to Texas A&M on a football scholarship, said that confidence was the most important factor in attaining success on the golf course, the football field or in any other area of sport.[1]

Arnold Palmer recognizes this fact, and has said so on a number of occasions. In one magazine article in which he was talking about the intangibles of golf he said confidence was the most important single factor of them all. He himself is one of the game's prime examples of confidence in action. His statement, "I never saw a hole I couldn't birdie" is characteristic of his approach to the game.

Lee Trevino is an example of how confidence helps to develop one's full potential. Many have pointed out the seeming awkwardness of his flat swing, yet he wins, and is at his best in major tournaments. His attitude is characterized by a remark he made about Nicklaus when being interviewed before the Open in '71. He recognized Nicklaus as the rightful favorite. He said he thought Nicklaus was the greatest golfer in the world. He said, "There's no one else like him." Then he added, "but I can beat him."

Psychologically we know that any attitude, any attribute may have many causes, many explanations and may come from many different sources. This is no less true of confidence. It can be the result of many causes. It can have many explanations. The roots of confidence, like those of any other behavior, are multiple, complex and inter-related.

What are some of the things that successful golfers have done or thought that gives them confidence? In one sense every other section of this study contributes to confidence.

Confidence comes with a knowledge and mastery of the fundamentals. It does not replace them. One can have all the confidence in the world but if his grip is faulty he will still hook or slice. On the other hand, a knowledge of how to hit good shots makes one confident. We can only be confident if we know what we are doing.

Confidence comes with practice. The good players have practiced so much they have attained the feel of a good swing. They know they can make a shot because they have made so many in practice. It is said of Henry Picard that he used to practice his irons from dawn to dusk. He became so confident of his shots to the green that he told a friend that he felt each shot might go into the hole.[2]

Whenever the good golfers experience a slump or a bad round, this is their first move—back to the practice tee. Hitting ball after ball, they regain their timing, renew their sense of feel and restore their confidence.

So important is this matter of confidence the pros will do almost anything to attain it or maintain it. Frank Beard tells of an experience with Gary Player which illustrates this point. They were playing at Greensboro and Beard saw Player on the practice green practicing 18 inch putts. He had 100 balls and was putting one after another in the hole.

"What are you practicing for?" Beard asked, "Obviously you never miss them."

"That's right," he (Player) said, "but I'll tell you what. The greatest thing for putting is confidence. And the greatest thing for confidence is watching that ball go in the hole. I'll stand here until my confidence is high. The subconscious is watching that ball go in the hole."(3)

Gene Littler felt the importance of confidence so much he paid a psychologist $700.00 for a motivational course that would help him attain it.

Confidence comes with experience. Palmer feels he can play well because he has played well. It is too much to expect the beginner to feel confident right away. Doug Ford once said, "Confidence without ability is difficult to maintain." Confidence without experience is impossible to secure.

This is perhaps one explanation for the amazing record of Jack Nicklaus. He began playing when he was ten. He won his first tournament when he was thirteen. He experienced success so young that confidence was almost there from the beginning. When he was sixteen he won the Ohio State Open and qualified for the U.S. Open. When he was nineteen he played on the Walker Cup team in Scotland and was invited to the Masters. When he was only twenty he recorded the lowest score ever made by an amateur in the U.S. Open and might have won it except for Palmer's dramatic charge from six strokes back. When he was twenty one he won the U.S. amateur and then turned pro.

When Nicklaus entered the professional ranks the game was dominated by some colorful and highly successful competitors. Nicklaus respected them but was never over-awed by them. He had a quiet confidence that he could compete with them and did—in fact he won the Open the first time he played in it as a pro. He had all the strokes from the beginning, but a lot of skilled young men have had the strokes—he had the confidence to go with them.

All golfers agree that confidence comes with confident thinking. A player has to think confidently to play confidently. This is the emphasis on positive concentration all over again. Lee Trevino says, "I drive straighter than anybody, so the more trouble there is the better I like it." In the 1971 P.G.A. Dave Stockton led going into the last round with Arnold Palmer in second. When asked how he felt Stockton said, "Nobody can putt and chip better than I can. . .I just feel like I'm going to win." The next day he scrambled in and out of the bunkers, the woods, even the water, but he putted and chipped as well as anyone and won his first major tournament.

These statements of Trevino and Stockton were not conceit. They had confidence and it produced results.

Most golfers have had to acquire confidence over a period of time. Few have had the early success that Nicklaus had. In fact few have even approached it. Hogan, for example, had great confidence and one of the greatest swings of all time. He played with a coolness and a confidence that was even a marvel to the Scots who coined the phrase "the wee Ice Mon."

Of the two, the swing and the confidence, he attained the swing first. Even after he had a swing that would win tournaments, he still had periods of uncertainty. He describes how it happened. "I never felt genuinely confident about my game until 1946. Up to that year, while I knew once I was on the course and playing well that I had the stuff that day to make a good showing, before a round I had no idea whether I'd be 69 or 79. I felt my game might go sour on any given morning. I had no assurance that if I was a little off my best form I could still produce a respectable round. My friends on the tour used to tell me that I was silly to worry, that I had a grooved swing. . .But my self-doubting never stopped. Regardless of how well I was going, I was still concerned about the next day and the next.

"In 1946 my attitude suddenly changed. I honestly began to feel that I could count on playing fairly well each time I went out, that there was no practical reason for me to feel I might suddenly 'lose it all'. I would guess that what lay behind my new confidence was this: I had stopped trying to do a great many difficult things perfectly because it had become clear in my mind that this ambitious over-thoroughness was neither possible nor advisable, or even necessary. All you needed to groove were the fundamental movements—and there weren't so many of them. . .I don't know what came first, the chicken or the egg, but at about the same time I began to feel that I had the stuff to play creditable golf even when I was not at my best, my shot making started to take on a new and more stable consistency."[4]

Confidence like any other attitude must be learned; it is a result of many influences, but all the good golfers agree—confidence is the name of the game.

(1) cf Nicklaus, *Never Say Never,* Fleet Publishing Company, 1965, p. 5.

(2) cf Nieporte and Sauer: *Mind Over Golf,* Doubleday, 1968, p. 25.

(3) Beard, *Saving Strokes With Frank Beard,* Grosset and Dunlap, 1969, p. 23.

(4) Hogan: *The Modern Fundamentals of Golf,* A. S. Barnes, 1957, p. 113.

# 13

# The Mental Side Of Putting

*All the experts agree that the mental side of putting is at least equal to, if not more important than, the mechanical.*

The putter is the only club that is used on every hole. The only exception would be if a person chips in an approach shot or makes a hole in one. Therefore most pros would say it is the most important club in the bag. If a person is playing poorly but putting well he can still have a pretty good round. The opposite may not necessarily be true. If he is playing well but putting poorly his score may not reflect his good play.

Since most courses have a par of 71 or 72, and since one is alloted 36 putts for regulation par, it is with real justification that Arnold Palmer can say, "Putting is half of the game."(1)

Anyone who has watched the pros at a tournament or on television knows that there is nothing in golf where there is more variation than in putting. One can see almost anything on a putting green. Some men use blade putters; some use mallet heads; some prefer steel shafts, some glass, and some cling to the old wooden shafted models. Somc men putt hunched over like Nicklaus; some knockkneed like Palmer;

**Sooner or later it all comes down to putting—putting comes down to the attitudes of the one holding the putter**

some putt cross-handed like Johnny Pott; some with hands wide apart like Phil Rodgers. Some are fast like Boros; some slow and meticulous like Player. Some excellent putters prefer to stroke the putt, some would rather tap it. Billy Casper, one of the best of them all, strokes the long putts but taps the short ones. Hogan, speaking of a putting style, says it is like choosing a wife, "to each his own."

Tom Michael and the editors of *Golf Digest* produced a book on putting entitled *Golf's Winning Stroke* in which they said this is one aspect of the game anyone can do well. They said, "There is no compelling reason why any normal golfer can't learn to putt as well as a professional, provided he has the time to devote to developing sound putting techniques. Having a positive mental attitude about your ability to do so is a most important starting point."(2) Bud Caskill, teaching pro, in a little book *Golf at a Glance* says putting is one half mental and one half swing.(3)

The pros are in pretty much agreement about the mechanics of putting. The head must be still and the body steady. The eyes must be over the ball, the blade of the putter must be square to the line to the hole, the stroke must always be an accelerating stroke. If these basics are present one can allow for all the variation he wants. The stance can be open, closed or square—no matter. The grip can be standard, reverse overlap, or cross-handed—no matter—as long as the putter returns square to the hole. The main thing—whatever the stance—the person must feel comfortable and the stroke must accelerate.

The rest is mental. It is what one thinks about when putting that is important. On this all the experts agree. The most important single ingredient of good putting is confidence. All the methods of directing one's thoughts are to produce confidence.

Much has been said about putters. All sorts are used. Some men stay with one putter over the years, others change several times a season. When all has been said, done and experimented with it is the stroke and the attitude that count. If one learns the basic fundamentals of putting and has a confident attitude he can putt with any putter. In a tournament in 1972 Bob Rosburg, who has both of the above, leaned on his putter and broke the shaft. He had to finish the last three holes putting with a three iron. He one putted all three greens.

The pros suggest two methods of lining up long putts. One is the "imaginary circle" method advocated by Jack Nicklaus. In this one visualizes a circle of three or four feet in diameter, with the cup in the center. One then putts for this larger circle. The other is the "strive for perfection" method of Cary Middlecoff. He says, "Why not try for perfection? It costs no more. . .The whole point is that the best way to get close is to try to get in." [4] Both are trying to accomplish the same thing. They are trying to build up confidence.

Many pros advocate visualizing a line to the hole (see section on visualization). Some suggest selecting a spot on the green one third to one half the distance on the line and putting for that spot, Player suggests selecting a spot much closer to the ball. He feels one should select a spot not more than a foot away that will be on the right line and then hit the ball over that spot. This gets the ball started right and

Lee Trevino expects to make his putts

since the spot is so close it builds confidence.[5] On short putts some suggest visualizing a path the width of the cup back to the ball, then putting down that path.

All pros are experts at reading the greens. They point out that they pay more attention to the break within four feet of the cup than any place else. However, having read the green, most of them point out that it is more difficult to judge distance than to read the green. On long putts most people miss farther by being short or long than they do by being too much to the right or left. For this reason they advocate that one's concentration should be more on distance than on line. Casper says, "The emphasis on long putts should always be on the stroking speed."

There is a difference of opinion as to whether one should think of putting past the hole, or of thinking of putting just to reach the hole. On the premise that you can't make it if you don't reach it, some advocate thinking of putting just beyond the hole. If it does go past, you know the break and can putt coming back. Others say a slow putt that just arrives at the hole has four chances of dropping in—front, right, left and back. For this reason Middlecoff says one should putt so that the ball drops in the hole on the last turn.[6] All agree that one should putt so that if he misses it will be on the high (or pro) side of the cup. This gives the ball an extra chance.

All such suggestions are to increase confidence. Hogan, in his first book of golf instruction *Power Golf,* said the three key words of putting are concentration, relaxation and confidence.[7] Billy Casper says that the two most important factors in putting are for the golfer to be "comfortable and be confident." He also says you must always think of how you can "make" the putt, never how you can "miss" it. "It is surprising," he says, "how many putts you will make if you think you will." Middlecoff is stressing the same thing when he says, "Think of the way you're going to make the putt. That's all that should interest you. Nothing else counts. . . Always say to yourself, I'm going to hit this putt along this line and I intend to make it."[8] Palmer, whose success is at least partially due to his unlimited confidence, says, "When you walk up to a putt expecting to miss it, you do." But he also says, "If you think you're a good putter, if you keep telling yourself how great you are, it certainly helps."

In practice or play, be confident, think in terms of the way to make the putt, keep the head steady and knock it in.

(1) cf Palmer: *My Game and Yours,* Simon and Schuster, 1963, p. 112.

(2) Michael: *Golf's Winning Stroke,* Coward McCann, 1967, p. 25.

(3) cf Caskill, *Golf at a Glance,* A. R. C. Books, Inc., 1966.

(4) cf Michael, Ibid., p. 33.

(5) cf Player: *124 Golf Lessons,* Follett Publishing Company, 1967, p. 24.

(6) cf Middlecoff: *Advanced Golf,* Prentice Hall, 1957, p. 58.

(7) cf Hogan: *Power Golf,* A. S. Barnes, 1948, p. 130.

(8) Middlecoff, Ibid., p. 135.

**Bobby Jones and Calamity Jane won victories through skill and patience**

# 14

# Distractions Need Not Distract

*Most successful golfers agree that distractions must be accepted and ignored.*

Of all the advice that the experts give, this is probably the one they find the most difficult to apply themselves. Golfers have been known to be distracted by the click of a camera, the whisper of a broadcaster's voice, a cough in the gallery, the buzzing of a few gnats, or a fly landing on the ball. Raymond Floyd was so disturbed by a playing partner's slow play in a tournament that he said things for which he later apologized. Several pros have objected to Chi Chi Rodriguez's victory dance when he sinks a long putt.

Other athletes—notably baseball, basketball and football players—expect not only noise but taunts from the crowd and attempts by the opposition to distract or disconcert them. Not so with golfers. Some give the impression they would like to play on a sound-proof course where the weather is always constant. The truth is that golf is played with other people, on all kinds of courses, in all kinds of weather. Tournament golf is played before large groups of people, often numbering in the thousands, many of whom are no

Some distractions are hard to ignore, but Doug Sanders is trying

more than a club length away. Combine this with the sounds of traffic, airplanes and helicopters overhead, volunteer marshals, and all the other variables that surround a golf match, and some distractions are inevitable.

Things that are distractions to some serve as a challenge to others. The crowds which continually surround Arnold Palmer can be very distracting to his playing partners but they only make him play better.

The capacity to ignore distractions and continue one's concentration or forget incidents that have been distracting and continue to play one's game may be the difference in a good round and a bad one.

Bobby Jones in his early career was noted for his outbursts of temper. This has been discussed elsewhere in these pages. He not only developed the capacity to ignore distractions but he did it in such a way that it neither spoiled his game or his manners. He was playing in the British Open at St. Anne's in 1926. He was tied with Al Watrous on the 16th hole. He approached his ball and got set for a shot when someone with a camera stepped out and snapped it. Jones stepped back, resumed his stance and the man did it again. This time the crowd literally forced the man out of the way. Jones pitched to the green and got his par. Such a display of self-control would do credit to a man who had had no problems with his temper. Jones, who admitted it took a long time to develop such poise, handled the distraction both as a champion and as a gentleman.

Some have had to continue in the presence of rather unusual distracting situations. When Gary Player came to the U.S. to play in several tournaments in 1969 and '70 he was threatened by some groups who were protesting the apartheid policy of his native South Africa. At one tournament play was interrupted when some people broke through the gallery and ran at him. During the 1970 tour armed guards moved throughout the crowd to protect him from further incidents, even from bodily harm. Even so, he played some of the best golf of his career.

The black players, like Charlie Sifford, Lee Elder, and Pete Brown, have had problems not experienced by white players. Golf is one of the last sports to break the color line. Golf tournaments are usually played on country club courses and country clubs are probably the most segregated institutions in society. Now tournaments are open to the blacks who can qualify and incidents are much less frequent than they once were. They did, and occasionally still do, occur. In the Memphis Open of 1969 some spectators grabbed Lee Elder's tee shot and threw it in the bushes. Terry Dill, his playing partner, protested and Elder was granted a free drop. There were some jeers from the gallery.

Elder said, "People like this are in a small minority. If I lower myself to his level it will do more harm than good. . ." He took his shot and finished with a 67. To be able to play, and play so well in spite of such unfair and bigoted incidents, is a credit to their courage, skill, sportsmanship, and their amazing capacity to concentrate in spite of distractions that are unfair and regrettable.

Such patience finally paid off in '74 when he won the Monsanto Open and became the first black player to be invited to the Masters.

Some distractions may be due to the weather. Julius Boros' smooth swing and even temperament have resulted in one of the best records on the tour. There may be some significance to the fact that two of his biggest wins, the Open in 1963, and the P.G.A. at San Antonio in 1968, were both played in very adverse weather conditions. The Open at Brookline was played in extremely disconcerting wind. Boros refused to let it bother him and at 43 became the oldest man ever to win the Open. Five years later at San Antonio the heat was intense. The weather and the course took their toll. Such golfers as Tom Weiskopf and Jack Nicklaus failed to make the cut.

Boros wearing a floppy hat, carrying an umbrella for the sun, said the heat helped his bad back. He not only withstood the heat but the charge of Arnold Palmer who was standing in the fairway waiting while Boros calmly lined up a long putt, and in a characteristic fashion, without wasting any time, stroked it in to become the oldest man ever to win a major tournament.

Tommy Bolt theorizes that one reason professional golfers have so much concern with distractions is that most golfers developed their swings on "lonesome practice ranges" where there is little, if any, noise, no crowds, no cameras, no distractions of any kind. They learn to play, he says, in these surroundings, then they take their game to tournament competition and it is a totally different set of circumstances.

For the professional distractions are likely to come from the gallery. For the amateur they are of a different sort, but they are distractions nonetheless and they can appear from unexpected places. Bolt tells of playing a friendly game with three amateurs. A maintenance worker was driving a tractor near by pulling some gang mowers. The noise was fairly loud but constant. Three players hit to the green with no difficulty. Just as the fourth player started his down swing the workman cut off his motor. The result was disastrous. Tommy Bolt's comments are appropros whether it is the professional playing before an enthusiastic gallery or the amateur contending with whatever is the cause. He said there is only one thing you can control, that is swinging the golf club. The key is to concentrate on that, not on something you can't control.(1)

In the 1971 National Invitational at Colonial in Fort Worth, Lee Trevino was lining up his second shot on the 17th fairway. A helicopter descended and landed on the adjoining 15th fairway not more than 75 yards from where Trevino was standing. It scattered the crowd, sent the marshals scurrying to see what was the situation. Trevino waited until the pilot turned off the motors then drilled his shot to the center of the green. The marshals were more distracted than Trevino was.

The course itself can be distracting. Gary Player says one must make friends with a course. He contends that when a person begins to complain that the course is too difficult, or unfair, or not well maintained then one begins to think negatively; he expects bad shots and consequently doesn't play well. He cited Walter Hagen, who never seemed to worry or complain about a course. He knew his opponents had to play the same course so he went ahead and played.

Perhaps no golf course has been subjected to so much criticism as Hazeltine in Minnesota, the site of the 1970 Open. Dave Hill was fined $150.00 for a comment critical of the course. When he asked what he felt the course needed he said a few acres of corn and some cows. Some feel that one reason some of the pros played it so poorly was that they had such a negative attitude toward it to start with.

In contrast Tony Jacklin, the winner by seven strokes, made no complaints. "I just try to accept things as they are," he said. "The course isn't going to change so you might as well try to accept it."–which is true of most distractions.

(1) cf Bolt: *The Hole Truth*, J. P. Lippincott, 1971, p. 49.

Chi Chi laments a bad round (but he's had many good ones)

# 15

# Some Bad Shots Are Inevitable

*The experts say that bad shots should be expected, accepted, and forgotten.*

Even the best golfers hit a bad shot once in awhile. Gene Littler was playing in the National Invitation at Colonial in Fort Worth. He was in contention when he came to the ninth hole on the final day. It is a short par four which requires a well placed drive, a short pitch across a narrow pond guarding the green for a par or a possible bird. Littler's swing is so smooth it is almost automatic. He hit a good drive and was in good position. The pin was fairly close to the pond. He cut it a little close and landed in the water. He dropped another ball and did the same thing. He could stand there all day and never hit another one into the pond, but this time he did.

Jack Nicklaus may be the best driver that ever played the game but even he hooks one out of bounds once in awhile. In the 1961 Masters Palmer needed a four on the last hole to win, a bogey to tie. His drive left him 150 yards from the hole. It appeared to be a cinch. A carelcss seven iron landed in the sand. Too clean a shot out of the sand sailed clear over the green. A pitch and a missed putt resulted in a six and a tie for second.

Such incidents should be some comfort to the average golfer. The question is, "What do the experts advise about bad shots and one's attitude toward them?" The first thing one would recognize is that they expect them. Walter Hagen used to say he assumed at the outset of a round that he would hit three or four bad shots, so he was psychologically prepared to take them in stride. Julius Boros says the same thing. He says he knows when he leaves the club house there will be some bad shots, so he accepts them. In the PGA at San Antonio on the third day, before a national television audience, he missed a putt of less than a foot. In characteristic fashion he said, "One putt doesn't make a tournament"; he kept on and won.

There is a lesson here for the amateur. We discussed this with a caddy at Royal Birkdale outside Liverpool. He had caddied for many years, including the Ryder Cup matches, the British Open, as well as for thousands of amateurs. We asked him what was the biggest problem he had with people he had carried for. He said it was people who think every shot should be perfect and get all upset if they miss one.

Gary Player says he expects two bad shots a round. He says a scratch golfer should expect five bad shots without "cursing his form", and a handicap golfer more. He says, "I reason this way. The same scratch player is entitled to expect two good chip shots, a good bunker shot, and two putts that drop but could just as easily have stayed out. In this way the balance is restored to his game. If he keeps his head and does not become upset at his lapses, he will be in a position to take advantage of his luck. If he allows his game to disintegrate, however, all the luck in the world later on will not help."(1) He also admits that this is one of the most difficult lessons that golfers have to learn.

Alfred Adler, the great psychologist, used to speak about the "courage of imperfection." He wasn't talking about golf, but it applies here. Billy Casper has said that if he hits half a dozen shots that come off the way he planned them he feels he has done pretty well.

Once a person has hit a bad shot, or gets a bad bounce, then he needs to take himself in hand. One bad shot must not be permitted to cause a second or third. Walter Hagen probably hit as many bad shots as any successful golfer. Arthur Crome, the British golf writer, said Hagen hit more bad shots in a season than Vardon hit in his whole career but Hagen still won because he didn't let it upset him. He knew he could hit good shots because he had and, as Crome said,

**(Even the good ones hit bad shots once in awhile.) Lee Trevino tosses down his club, Dave Stockton registers dissatisfaction, and Frank Beard is afraid to look.**

he knew that three of "those" and one of "them" still made four.

Frank Beard speaking of temperament says, "Most people–like me–hit one bad shot and start thinking about it, and then they hit another. So much of this game is control, concentration and control."(2)

John Jacobs, who was himself a successful tournament player in England and also one of Britain's most successful teachers, distinguishes between "playing" and "competing". He says too many golfers try for perfection and get discouraged when they are striking the ball poorly. A good competitor, however, will continue to bear down and even win when he is not hitting the ball too well. In his judgment, even the best golfers only hit six or seven shots a round that are exactly what they want, but they are competitors. They don't get discouraged by the shots that are not what they had expected or hoped for.(3)

Bruce Devlin says one of the main secrets of scoring well is to be able to "shrug off setbacks." Some feel one reason for his success is his ability to forget a bad hole or a bad shot.(4) Tommy Armour said that when you have hit a bad shot do not try to think about what you did wrong. Concentrate only on the next shot and what you should do right.

George Archer speaking of pressure says it takes time to learn to live with it and control it. "You learn over the years that nobody is going to strike you dead if you blow a shot."

Julius Boros put it all into perspective for the amateur when he said, "What if you do knock it into the trap? Your life doesn't depend on it. Not even your living."

(1) Scott: *Secrets of the Golfing Greats,* A. S. Barnes, 1965, p. 43.

(2) Beard: *Pro: Frank Beard on the Golf Tour,* Bantam Books, 1970, p. 69.

(3) cf Jacobs: *Practical Golf,* Quadrangle Books, 1972, p. 144.

(4) cf Devlin: *Play Like the Devil,* Doubleday, 1970, p. 139.

# 16

# Overcome Bad Rounds With Good Attitudes

*Most of the experts advise that when one is having a bad round, he should just keep swinging.*

A wise man once said, "Obstacles are things to be overcome." The same thing can be said about a bad round of golf.

The idea of a bad round is relative. What is a bad round for Nicklaus would be an excellent round for most golfers. What we mean by a bad round here is one that is poorer than one customarily plays.

Even the best golfers have bad rounds, sometimes several in a row. In 1965 Palmer went eleven months without winning a tournament, and in 1970-71 he went even longer until he won the Bob Hope Classic in the spring of 1971. There must have been several rounds in that period of time that were poorer than he customarily plays; in fact, he missed the cut for the Open by two strokes.

Anyone who follows the weekly scores of the tour in the papers knows that some excellent golfers have some bad rounds. It is not uncommon for a golfer to win a tournament one week and not make the cut the next. In the spring of 1971 Bob Shaw won the Bing Crosby and failed to make the cut at Phoenix the next week. He came back to win the Hawaiian Open and became the leading money winner on the tour for awhile, but failed to make the cut at the PGA.

Gene Littler said it can be very discouraging to go weeks at a time, not making many good shots. They, too, know the experience.

Even Nicklaus, who may well be the best golfer in the world today, is not exempt. In the 1970 Open at Hazeltine he had an 81 in the opening round. For a man who averages 70 or below, that is a pretty poor round, especially in a tournament he had intended to win, according to a statement he made in a national magazine.

The experts have some common advice to give about such occasions. The first is to keep on swinging to the end of the round. Sam Snead once said, "Never give up on a hole." The same thing could be said about a round. Gary Player has frequently said one should never give up on a round no matter how he is scoring.

Jack Nicklaus began the 1971 PGA playing very poorly, for him. He was very much determined, however, and kept on and, by one-putting eight of the last ten greens he turned what Dan Jenkins said could easily have been a 76 into a 69 and took the lead. He simply refused to give up.

Bob Goalby almost gave up on a whole tournament. He was playing in the Sahara Invitational in Las Vegas. He had a 71 and a 75 on the first two rounds and assumed that 146 would not make the cut. He packed his bags, went to the airport and even got on the plane. Then it occurred to him that the bumpy greens and the strong winds might have caused some other fellows to have troubles, too. He got off the plane, phoned the course, and found that he was still eligible for the final two rounds. He went back to the course, shot a pair of 66's on the final two days, tied for second, and won $7,733.00.(1)

Whether it is a hole, a round or a tournament, the experts agree: never give up. Al Geiberger says, "Many players don't give themselves a chance after a bad break or a few bad holes and become upset. They forget that they're playing eighteen or seventy-two holes and that a lot of good can happen on the remaining holes." Tom Nieporte says basically the same thing, "It means simply that a player must learn to wait when he scores poorly or makes an error in judgment. Success will come if he is resilient and retains his composure."[2]

Lee Trevino, playing in the 1971 Sahara Invitational at Las Vegas, was attempting to become the leading money winner. On the first day, in bitter cold weather, though bundled up in a sweater and rain gear, he shot a 69 to be one stroke back in second place. He gained the lead on Friday, but Saturday a 73 put him in fourth place, four shots back. Shortly after finishing the round he said, "I've forgotten that 73 already . . .Tomorrow I'm coming back, shoot a 66 and either win or finish second." That's forgetting a bad round. The next day he shot a 66 and won.

A second thing the experts would say about a bad round is: Don't experiment while on the course. The place for that is on the practice tee. Also don't take advice from an amateur. There may be exceptions when a friend who is familiar with one's game can detect a flaw or the need for a change, but usually it is better to seek advice from a pro, not an average golfer.

After the round is the time to seek the advice of a pro and the time to go to a practice tee. Often a very slight adjustment will produce a dramatic change and a session or two on the practice tee will bring one's timing back.

We mentioned the fact that even Palmer has had occasions when he wasn't playing well. He has been very candid about this in his articles in the golf journals and in his books. He recognizes that it is both a physical and psychological problem. When one's game slips a bit out of its groove, probably because of a lack of concentration, then one's confidence is shaken, too. His advice is simple, yet profound and optimistic. It is "keep swinging". He says if you maintain your confidence, don't let the game get the best of you, keep on swinging, pretty soon things fall in place again.[3]

John Jacobs says what separates the good golfer from the average golfer, or what enables a man to compete as well as just play golf is "confidence in one's self, and a relentless determination to keep trying whatever happens."(4)

(1) cf *Golf Magazine,* March 1971, p. 21.

(2) Nieporte & Sauer: *Mind Over Golf,* Doubleday, 1968, p. 17.

(3) cf Palmer: *My Game and Yours,* Simon and Schuster, 1963, p. 60, 61.

(4) Jacobs: *Practical Golf,* Quadrangle Books, 1972, p. 144.

# 17

# Good Shots Can Pick You Up Or Let You Down

*The successful golfers say that after an especially good shot, one should enjoy it, forget it, and concentrate on the next shot.*

Nothing is more enjoyable than a good golf shot. That is why so many people play the game. It may be a drive that splits the fairway, an iron that spins to a stop in the middle of the green, a chip shot that nestles close to the pin for a birdie putt—no difference—it is a thing of beauty and a real accomplishment. One of the fascinating things about golf is that even a poor golfer can hit a good shot once in awhile.

There have been some great shots in the history of golf. Gene Sarazen's double eagle on the 15th at Augusta in the final round of the Masters is one of the most frequently described. It was a four wood over the water, onto the green and into the hole. Every spring as the sports writers begin to drum up interest in the Masters that shot is redescribed. Hogan's two iron on the last hole of the Open at Merion is another that is remembered and discussed over and over. There have been many others such as Jerry Barber's long putts, the width of the green, to win the PGA.

Every tournament produces some amazing shots. We remember seeing Jack Nicklaus hit a seven iron off a concrete walking bridge over a bank of trees onto the green to get a par on 18 at Colonial. He didn't win the tournament but that impossible shot was worth the price of admission.

Strange as it may seem, one can be vulnerable after such an experience. Dave Stockton was leading the final round of the 1970 PGA at Tulsa. He was paired with Arnold Palmer, his closest competitor. Stockton got an eagle, and then promptly took a double bogey on the next hole.

On the final day of the 1971 Colonial he holed out a shot from the sand on number two. It was a fantastic shot for a birdie. On the next hole he pushed one out of bounds.

On the first day of the 1972 Masters, Charles Coody the defending champion, had a hole in one with a five iron on the 190 yard sixth hole. On the 7th he had a triple bogey when he stayed in a sand trap for three shots. He went from a one to a seven in two holes which caused his friend Frank Beard to comment that it was a strange way to get an 8 for two holes.

Frank Beard had a similar experience himself. In his account of life on the tour he describes an incident that occurred in the very first tournament of the year. He parred the first hole. He hit a good drive and four wood to six feet of the pin on the second hole. He got his bird and hit a three-iron to within three feet of the pin on the 3rd, a par three 208 yard hole. He describes it in this fashion. "I was two under after three holes, and most people come through those holes one over par. I figured I had the world by the tail. I was walking around like I was on stage, like the cock of the walk. I lost my concentration.

"Next thing I knew, I put a drive over in the trees on an easy birdie hole. I was still thinking about my two great birdies and I hooked, and all I could do was pitch out and pitch up on the green and take two putts for a bogey."(1)

Even a successful shot can break the concentration. Notice how many times a bogey follows a birdie among average players. One should not still be relishing a shot on the last hole when he should be concentrating on the shot at hand. Some of the experts suggest that just as one should take a little time and let the emotions subside after hitting a bad shot, he should do the same thing after hitting a good shot.(2)

It is also true that a good shot can pick a man up and restore his confidence. Many times when players recount how they won a tournament they will point back to one particular shot that came at the right time which they say turned the tide, or gave them new confidence. Olin Dutra won the U.S. Open at Merion in 1934 in a memorable duel with Gene Sarazen. Sarazen had beaten him two years before at Fresh Meadow, N.Y., when he played the last 28 holes in 100 strokes or for an average of 3.16 per hole. Sarazen was on the frog hair in two at 18 when Dutra was playing 15. Dutra had a long putt on a slick green. In order to be able to see over the crowd Sarazen climbed on his caddy's back.

Dutra studied the green from every direction. He described the shot in an interview with Bob Scharf of *Golf* magazine. "The greens were like putting on a mahogany table. I took one last look, then, plunk, it went into the hole. A birdie. Gene fell off his caddy's back and went over and took three to get down from the fringe. . ." That shot did it, he said. He went on to win by one stroke.(3)

In the 1971 PGA Nicklaus was not playing well but by concentration and superb putting he maintained his lead. He was challenged first by Gary Player and then by Casper. A long birdie putt however and he said he knew he had it. That shot picked him up, increased his confidence, improved his play.

The possibility of a good shot should keep a person going until there is no more chance to score. There is an old saying that "it only takes one good shot to par a hole." It may be a good drive that puts one in position. It may be a good recovery shot that gets one out of trouble. It may be a long putt that snakes across the green and falls in the hole. As long as there is that possibility there is a chance. That's when Palmer says you have to "reach inside yourself" and make a shot that is better than you can play.

In the 1971 Colonial at Fort Worth Gene Littler was not playing very well. He came to the 18th tee on the third day well down in the pack. He said at that point if some one would have given him $500.00 and a ticket to California he would have taken it and gone home. However he hit a good drive, pitched in a perfect approach shot for an eagle. The next day he continued with a good solid performance. It was a wild, windy day. Some very fine golfers found the wind and a very tough golf course difficult to cope with. Littler shot a good steady "one under" for the round, passed a whole group who were above him and won $25,000.00. All of which demonstrates two things. A good shot can pick a person up and turn things around, and if a person keeps plugging away at a steady pace some good things will happen.

The year Bobby Nichols won the P.G.A. he was in trouble all afternoon of the final round. But good recovery shots kept saving the day.

The good golfers let the good shots increase their confidence and they put a whole series of them together. There have been some great instances of this. Byron Nelson and Ben Hogan, both from the caddy ranks of Fort Worth, tied for the 1942 Masters. They met in a playoff the next day. Nelson double bogeyed the first hole and bogeyed the 4th. Hogan had him three down as they came to the sixth tee. In the next eleven holes Nelson birdied the 6th, parred the 7th, eagled the 8th, which really charged him up, birdied the 11th, 12th and 13th. In the same eleven holes Hogan was one under par and lost five strokes.

In the 1967 Masters Hogan himself gave one of the greatest demonstrations of fine shots ever seen and he was almost 55 years old. It was one of his rare competitive appearances. He hit 17 of 18 greens in regulation and had a 66 for the day, which was the low round of the week. It was the back nine which was the masterpiece of good shot making. He played the last nine with six birdies and three pars, what Dan Jenkins of *Sports Illustrated* called the "most elegant shot making ever in a major tournament." He played "without a single error in judgement or technique, without a single fairway miss or a putt of more than twenty feet. . ." When he came up to the 18th green he received as extended a round of applause as anyone has ever received on a golf course.(4)

As long as good shots are made golf will be fun to watch and play. There is always the possibility the next one will be better.

(1) Beard: *Pro: Frank Beard on the Golf Tour,* Bantam Books, 1970, p. 27.
(2) cf Nieporte: *Mind Over Golf,* Doubleday, 1968, p. 45.
(3) *Golf Magazine,* June 1971, p. 45.
(4) *Sports Illustrated,* April 7, 1969, p. 44.

**How sweet it is!**
**Rod Curl sinks a birdie putt at Colonial in '74 and went on to win his first tournament.**

# 18

# Good Rounds Are Their Own Reward

*The successful golfers say—during a good round, forget the consequences and play one shot at a time.*

Jack Nicklaus says there are two times when one must watch his mental attitudes, one is when he is playing badly, and the other is when he is playing well. The problems are different but they are nonetheless real. Strange as it may seem, when one is going well he may be subjected to certain pressures just as much as when he is having a bad day.

Frank Beard, the leading money winner of 1969, said that naturally he likes to lead a tournament but he also says, "I've got to admit. . .that the pressure of being in the lead is a lot greater than the pressure of coming from behind.

When one is having a good round he may get over-confident or over-cautious. Either one can lead to problems. When one is over-confident he lets up and makes a careless shot; when he is over-cautious he may change his tempo, miss a shot and often loses his momentum.

When one is playing well he may begin to think of a new record (for himself, the course, a tournament) and also lose his concentration. If he begins to think of the outcome, the

**Lee's caddy shares his exultation**

trophy, the final score, the same thing can happen. When his mind is turned to any of these possible outcomes he usually doesn't concentrate on the individual shots.

In the 1966 U.S. Open in San Francisco, Arnold Palmer led Billy Casper by seven strokes going into the final nine. The question seemed to be, not who would win the Open, but would Palmer break Hogan's record. How Casper made up the seven strokes to force it into a play-off the next day is common knowledge to all golf fans. The next day Casper won his second Open. His (Casper's) evaluation of what happened was that probably neither of them was thinking of the title. Palmer was thinking about Hogan's record and Casper was trying to protect second place. He was playing smoothly. Palmer took chances and got into trouble.

Ray Floyd was having a fantastic round in the 1970 P.G.A. at Tulsa. IIis putting was superb. Hc camc to the 18th hole needing only a short putt to have a 64 and a new course record. He had been making more difficult putts all day but he missed this one. Afterwards he told a newspaper reporter he guessed he was thinking about the record, not the putt. In the same tournament Dave Stockton had a comfortable margin going into the final holes. Dave Marr, a former P.G.A. winner himself, was doing commentary on TV. He said that one of Dave's problems would be to keep from making up acceptance speeches and to keep his mind on the shots at hand.

Tony Jacklin was in a similar position in the U.S. Open the same year. He entered the fourth round with a five stroke lead. He said he remembered how Palmer had blown a seven stroke lead to Casper in the same tournament four years before. He said he tried not to think that he was winning the Open, not to think of presentation ceremonies but just to play golf.

This is what Bobby Nichols means when he says, "Play the shot, not the event."

John Miller in the 1971 Masters had a good round going in the last day. He had a 33 on the front nine, birdied the 11th, 12th and 14th. "That was the first I thought about winning," he said. He decided to go for his birdie on 15. It meant he had to carry the water with a three wood. "I was standing there with the spoon in my hand, and I actually thought about how the green coat would look on me." By parring in he would have forced a play off. The way he had been playing this should have been easy. Perhaps the thought of that green coat spoiled his concentration. He bogeyed 16 and 18 while Charlie Coody birdied 15 and 16 and finished with two pars to win.

Apparently he learned his lesson for he won the U.S. Open in 1973 and started 1974 by winning the first three tournaments of the year (which was a new record) as well as two or three more.

The successful golfers remind us that if one starts thinking about the final score, the results of the round, or how well he is doing, he cannot concentrate on the shot. They are aware

**A job well done. Weiskopf pictures a sense of satisfaction as he recognizes the applause of the crowd.**

of what they are doing all the time, but they still play one shot at a time.

Golf has had many good rounds in its long history, and not a few great ones. Some stand out as monumental because they opened new eras in the game. This was true of Vardon's win in the U.S. Open in 1900, which introduced America to a new style of play. It was true of Francis Oimet's round in the Open fourteen years later when he defeated Vardon and Ted Ray in a triple play-off. The win of this eighteen-year-old Boston store clerk gave Americans a new interest in the game and a new confidence in their ability to compete with the British.

It was true of Bobby Jones' play in the 1930 U.S. Amateur which completed his grand slam. It was true of Hogan's last round 68 at Carnoustie in the British Open in 1953 to establish himself as the undisputed leader in the golfing world. It is impossible even to list the great rounds of golf—Hagen, Sarazen, Armour, Nelson, Snead, Palmer, Casper, Player, Weiskopf and Nicklaus all had them.

Every tournament produces some good rounds and an occasional great one. Every amateur who plays regularly and practices consistently will have a good round on occasion and, if he practices faithfully enough and develops the right attitudes along with a growing knowledge and mastery of the fundamentals, he may do so frequently.

A good round, whether on the first day of the Open or in a club championship, is a combination of many things. It is the fruitation of all one's previous practice and experience. It is a combination of controlled attitudes and applied skills. It may be a victory of patience and self-control. It is the result of wise management and intelligent choices. It is a demonstration of one's capacity to maintain poise under pressure. It probably represents the ability to recover from a mistake, to ignore distractions, to rise above disappointment, for there are few rounds without some such frustrations. It is evidence of one's capacity to maintain his confidence and pursue his goals without yielding to the temptations of good fortune or the discouragements of misfortune. It is a combination of physical skill, mental attitudes, disciplined thoughts, persistence and commitment. That is why golf is such a fascinating, intriguing and challenging game.

Every good round is a genuine achievement and, like virtue, it is its own reward.

# 19

# 'He That Controlleth His Own Spirit'

*Most successful golfers have learned to control their tempers as well as to control their swing.*

There is a bit of ancient wisdom which says,

"He who is slow to anger is better than the mighty,
And he who rules his spirit than he who takes a city."
–(Proverbs 16:32)

This was written centuries before golf was first played at St. Andrews but it is a lesson that every golfer must learn. Scott and Cousins in their book on the *Golf Immortals,* said, "The player who wants to win regularly at golf cannot afford to be affected by moods. He must be good as a general rule, brilliant on occasion, and capable of taking himself in hand very firmly and expertly if he happens to have an off day."(1)

There is no better example of this truth than in the great Bobby Jones himself. Bobby Jones probably had as much natural ability as anyone who ever played the game. He was one of those rare phenomena that come along once in a generation–a completely natural athlete. Joe DiMaggio and Willie Mays had it in baseball, Jesse Owens in track, Sammy

Baugh in football. All were natural athletes. They did so easily what others would strive for but could never quite attain. Sam Snead and Bobby Jones were both natural golfers.

Bobby Jones used his skills to win the U.S. Amateur five times, the U.S. Open four times, and on two other occasions tied and lost in the playoffs. He won the British Open three times and the British Amateur once. In 1930 he won all four in the same year, what the British sportswriters called "the impregnable quadrilateral" and the American sportswriters called the "grand slam". Then he retired at the age of 28.

No other amateur has ever approached his record, although Jack Nicklaus might have if he had not turned pro. Few professionals have approached it either.

One wouldn't expect a man with a record like that or with a swing which the authorities said didn't have a weakness to lose his temper. The week-end golfer, having trouble making solid contact with the ball, might well ask, "What did he have to lose his temper about?" The truth is that he did. All things are relative and Jones was just as dissatisfied with his game as the week-end golfer who takes a seven when he had hoped for a five. He was also just as quick to show his dissatisfaction—even to the extent of throwing his clubs on occasion.

In 1921, when he was playing in the third round of the British Open at St. Andrews, he found himself in a sand trap on the short 11th hole. Anyone who has played St. Andrews knows how difficult those traps can be. After failing twice to get out he tore up his card, walked off the course and out of the championship.

For years he had a personal caddy, until the U.S. Golf Association outlawed the practice. Luke Ross carried his clubs for six years and in twelve major championships. Years later, in an article in *Golf Digest,* Ross recalled how Jones in a fit of temper would throw his clubs and he (Ross) would have to retrieve them. He also noticed that after such an outburst he would usually hit another bad shot. Ross devised the strategy of returning very slowly when he had to go after a thrown club, thus giving Jones a chance to cool off.

Jones was a very intense person and played under great emotional strain. A friend who knew him at the time told how he scarcely could eat on the day of a match, and would become so nervous he could hardly button his shirt. He would sometimes become so nervous he would almost break into tears from the strain. In one tournament he lost eighteen pounds; during the 1925 Open he lost twelve pounds in three days.

He set for himself almost impossible goals and became furiously angry if he did not attain them. His anger was always directed at himself, not at his opponents or the course.

One reason for his amazing success and one that enabled him to utilize his fantastic natural ability was that he developed the capacity to control his emotions. He said he remembered something that was said about the great Harry Vardon. One of Vardon's greatest assets was the realization that no matter what happened there was only one thing he could do–keep hitting the ball. This he did. It took him a long time to attain such control but he did. "He stands forever," one sportswriter said, "as the greatest encourager of the highly strung player who is bent on conquering himself."

What was true of Jones was also true to a greater or less degree of most great golfers. There is an overworked phrase in sports, "He was his own worst enemy." It usually refers to a person who had great potential but didn't realize it until he learned to control his temper. This was true of Jones to a dramatic extent. It has also been true of many others whose improvement began when they took themselves in hand. It is also undoubtedly true that many golfers of great ability have not attained their full potential because they did not master their own tempers.

Tom Nieporte, who was both a winner on the tour and a good teaching pro, says, "A player who can't control his temper, who is easily upset by adversity, can't possibly play winning golf."[(2)]

There are many winning golfers whose success began when they began to control their tempers. Two of the most notable are Tommy Bolt and Bob Rosburg. Both have won national titles, both had to do battle with their own emotions. Bolt's tirades are legendary. He has been commonly referred to by sportswriters as the "terrible tempered Tommy Bolt" and as "thunder Bolt". Possessed of a beautiful swing, who knows how much he might have won. His record is impressive as it is. Bob Rosburg, whose appearance resembles that of a bank clerk as much as it does an athlete, doesn't look like one who would throw clubs, but there was a time when such a procedure cost him a good job. Let Nick Seitz tell it. "There was the time Rossie was being considered for the head professional job at an exclusive California club. He was playing a relaxed 18 holes with the president of the club and two influential members. Well, it was relaxed for everyone but Rossie.

"He hit a drive out of bounds. The stakes were something piddling like dollar-dollar-dollar, but with Rossie a bad shot is a bad shot, and he has never learned to tolerate one. He shouted a suggestive oath and flung his bag over a nearby fence. He did not get the job."

"Rossie's clubs have logged more air time than United," says Ken Venturi. The same article went on to tell how he had mellowed and won the Bob Hope Desert Classic, though 45 years of age.(3)

Much of the credit for Rosburg's control of his temper goes to his new wife who said, "I do a lot of reading of the world's religions and I just think there are a lot of things more important then missing a two foot putt."(4)

The test of one's ability to control his anger obviously comes when he gets in trouble. According to John Jacobs, British well-known teacher and former tournament player, this is inevitable. "Every golfer lands in trouble," he says. "How well he gets out depends on his mental equilibrium" as much as anything else. "Many golfers become so angry or dismayed when a bad miss lands them in cabbage that all reason departs. They call upon temper or belief in miracles to make amends. Neither are reliable factors in golf."(5)

George Archer who has won his share of tournaments said, "It has always been my feeling that you don't do yourself any good by a big display of anger or irritation. My idea is to keep your mouth shut and go hit the ball again."

Julius Boros, with the smooth swing and the smooth temperament is another who had to learn this lesson. His smooth, relaxed attitude was something he had to cultivate. "When I was younger," he says, "I was impatient like most kids. I threw a few clubs, bent some and broke some. I soon discovered that it didn't help anything and that it was pretty expensive. So I quit acting that way."(6)

An incident in his career illustrates how a positive application of this attitude helped him win his first Open championship in 1952. The tournament was being played in Dallas and Boros entered the final round with a two stroke lead on the field. He was still in the lead at the 12th when his tee shot found a trap to the left of the green. Boros is a great sand player, but on this occasion he left his first shot in the sand. The next one came out thirty-five feet from the pin. Two putts meant a double bogey and wiped out his lead. His comment later was, "I decided I still had a long way to go to get those two shots back if I just kept hitting the ball instead of the ceiling."(7) The ability to "hit the ball instead of the ceiling" is one secret of winning golf.

(1) *The Golf Immortals* by Tom Scott and Geoffrey Cousins, copyright 1969, Hart Publishing Company, Inc., N.Y.

(2) Nieporte and Sauer: *Mind Over Golf*, Doubleday, 1968, p. 11.

(3) *Golf Digest*, April 1972, p. 102.

(4) *Golf Magazine*, June 1972, p. 241.

(5) Jacobs: *Practical Golf*, Quadrangle Books, 1972, p. 99.

(6) *Great Golfers of the Twentieth Century*, Werner Book Cooperative, 1971, p. 66.

(7) Boros: *How to Play Golf With an Effortless Swing*, Prentice Hall, 1964, p. 21.

# 20

# Taking The Guesswork Out Of Club Selection

*The pros make whatever preparation possible that will take the guess work out of club selection.*

Bruce Devlin says, "Accuracy in club selection is at the very heart of good golf. . ."[1] The more one ponders this statement the more one realizes how true it is. Also the more one ponders it the more he becomes aware of how little attention the average player gives it. Not so the pros. They study their shots in practice and in play until they know precisely what club is needed for each occasion.

Cary Middlecoff said he never knew a great player who didn't make wise and precise club selections.

To make the right decision about a club, one must know what club will do for him. If a good player needs 165 yards to the center of the green, he must know what club will get him 165 yards. Tommy Bolt speaking of the uses of the various clubs says he knows the exact distances he can hit all the clubs, not the approximate distances.[2] Obviously this varies with the weather, the contour of the fairway, and especially with the wind.

Here we must go back to the section on visualization or imagery. John Jacobs, noted English golf teacher, speaking of the short game says, "You should never play a short shot until you have a clear mental picture of how you want the ball to behave. . .Until you decide how far and high the ball should fly, where it should land and how much it should roll, you cannot select the right club for the job." His advice is "picture the shot, then select the club that will match the picture."(3)

Charles Coody, "You can't think 6 iron and hit a good five iron."

The more the player knows what his clubs will do, the firmer the decision, the better the strategy, the more confident the swing. As Charles Coody said after he missed the green at a crucial point in the '69 Masters, "You can't hit a good five iron when you're thinking six iron."

Here is a good illustration of the very subtle relationship of the mental and mechanical aspects of golf. Cary Middlecoff, in his latest book entitled *The Golf Swing,* points out how a good golf swing depends on good golf strategy and club selection. A good golf swing, he contends, depends on having the mind cleared of all uncertainty, and confidence that the right plan has been formed and the right club selected to carry it out.(4)

The selection of the right club obviously depends on the ability to judge or estimate distance. When playing a familiar course this is not much of a problem. Memory of previous rounds serves as a guide. On some courses markers are placed at regular intervals to inform the golfer that he is 100, 150, or 200 yards from the green. During tournaments these mark-

Bobby Nichols selects the right club

ers are removed unless they happen to be bushes or trees that are placed at such distances.

Short distances (125 yards or less) can be paced off. Longer distances make this impractical, especially in these days when efforts are being made to speed up play. Even when markers are present one may find himself in a position where the distance is uncertain and the right club is of basic importance.

Some have developed a method of estimating distances to the green by selecting an object that is close and easy to estimate and then moving progressively by selecting other objects which he can see and adding the totals until he reaches the green. For example, one might select a tree or bush, or even a spot on the fairway that is about ten yards away, then another object ten yards from the first, and continue by jumps of ten yards until he has a fairly accurate estimate of the total yardage.

The pros point out that most players make the mistake of estimating the distance to the front of the green. Actually most greens are three club lengths long. It would be one club to the front of the green, another club to the middle, and perhaps even a third to reach the back of the green. The location of the pin would determine which of three clubs would be selected.

The pros who play different courses every week do not risk making mental estimates. They carefully pace off each hole during the practice rounds, noting the distance from the green of specific objects such as trees, bushes, the edge of a trap, etc. During play all they need to do is pace off the distance from this object (their marker) to the ball and add or subtract the difference. Jack Nicklaus practically catalogues a course and keeps a file on all the courses he has played. Billy Casper, who frankly admits his eyesight is poor and that he has trouble estimating distances, almost plots a course. All of this is, as Devlin says, to "take the guess work out of club selection."

Bob Lunn said, "I like to observe the whole course in a practice round. . .with utmost care. I want to know the position of the traps, the size of the greens, the distance to the greens from most any spot, the depth of the rough—how far it comes in (to the fairway), the distance from the tee to a bend of trees, the texture of the sand. . .a lot of things. These are things you have got to know to play good golf or passable golf. Whenever you go out and just hit the ball and keep your eye on the fairway ahead until again you hit, you're lost on the course. You're just playing around. You're not serious."(5)

When Gary Player was preparing for the 1965 United States Open he went to the course a week early. He not only played it, he mapped it, plotted it, diagrammed it. He noted distances, club selection from specific landmarks, trouble spots, and where he thought pin placements might be. After the practice rounds he would study the diagrams in his room and plan his strategy accordingly. During the tournament his caddy had a map of each hole ready when it was to be played. Player said his notebook turned out to be invaluable, for no matter where he was on the fairway, he knew exactly what club to use for his next shot. He was also familiar with how the ball rolled from various points on the green because he had practiced them and stepped it off.

A dramatic illustration of how a knowledge of the course can influence one occurred at the 1973 U.S. Open at Oakmont. Johnny Miller had a two under par 140 at the end of the second day. He was three shots behind Gary Player, the leader. The third day he forgot his yardage card and left it in his room. He shot a 76 and almost shot himself out of the tournament. The final day with his yardage chart to help him select his clubs he had a 63, the lowest round ever in the history of the Open. No one would contend that the yardage reminder produced the 63, but it is certain that its absence was in part responsible for the 76 and he couldn't have created a 63 without it.

(1) Devlin: *Play Like the Devil,* Doubleday, 1970, p. 68.

(2) cf Bolt: *The Hole Truth,* Lippincott, 1971, p. 76.

(3) Jacobs: *Practical Golf,* Quadrangle Books, 1971, p. 84.

(4) cf Middlecoff: *The Golf Swing,* Prentice Hall, 1969, p. 221.

(5) *Golf and Club,* March 1972.

# 21

# Think Your Way Around The Course

*All good golfers agree: To be a winner you must think your way around a golf course.*

On one of those rare occasions when Ben Hogan was a spectator at a golf tournament rather than a participant, he was asked to comment on the competitors and the influence of their swing on their standing. A good swing, he said, gives a man a twenty-five percent advantage, the rest is management.

What he called course management, some call strategy, others call it planning. Arnold Palmer in a recent publication calls it "situation golf."[(1)] No matter, it all means the same. It is the ability to think one's way around the golf course.

This is why Billy Casper says golf is a game of decisions. Each shot presents a variety of decisions. First of all what club to use, then how to use it. Does one play a hook, or a slice, a cut shot, or hit straight away? On most shots there is a question of whether one should play it safe or gamble. All of this is influenced by the lie, the condition of the course, the wind and weather and the status of the match.

The fact is that few golfers apply the strategy they know,

or utilize the knowledge that is available. Old pros like Cary Middlecoff stress this very strongly. He estimates that the difference in score between a player who uses good strategy and one who doesn't is about six strokes a round, if their abilities are equal. If he's only half right it would make a decided difference.(2)

This seems like a pretty large margin to give to management, but Tommy Armour who has taught, observed and played with all types of golfers divides it this way. He says those who shoot between par and 78 usually lose two strokes to poor planning; those in the 80's almost invariably toss away four shots "by not thinking golf", and he went so far as to say that those in the 90's could improve their game by ten strokes in the field of strategy alone. You can place yourself in your own category, compare it with Armour's estimate and you see the value of understanding course management.(3)

Jack Fleck, who upset Hogan to win the Open in 1955, said most golfers could improve their score if they would quit trying to play harder and just play smarter.

Successful golfers follow certain general principles on which they are in rather common agreement.

The first principle of golf management or strategy can be stated in five words, "Keep the ball in play." All else stems from this. On this point all winning golfers agree. Julius Boros has always played well in the Open. He has won two (1952 and 1963) and finished high in many others. When he won his first Open in Dallas he said his one objective was to keep the ball in play and go for pars. Even when he came down to the final round and was leading by two strokes he kept reminding himself that his job was to keep the ball in play, go for pars, and let the rest of the field shoot for him.(4)

Gene Littler was asked how he managed to win more than $700,000 while only playing a limited number of tournaments. He replied, "I've kept the ball in play pretty well. . .

that's the main reason I've won as much as I have the last 10 years."

A second principle is really an extension of the first, "Play away from trouble." This is absolutely necessary if one is to keep the ball in play. Most of the strategy on a golf course is determined by the hazards. That's why they are there. Golf courses are designed to provide alternates and force a golfer to make decisions and maneuver his way around hazards. Most problems can be avoided by planning and intelligent play.

**Ben Hogan plans a shot**

Billy Casper says, "From your tee shot on, you should carefully plan every swing to escape or avoid material and man made hazards and to place the ball in the most advantageous position for your next shot."(5)

Most pros tee the ball on the side nearest trouble and then aim away from it. This gives the whole fairway for a target and offers a much wider margin of error. When hazards are located in front of the green they play long; when they are behind the green they play short; when the pin is behind a trap they go for the center of the green. The smarter the player the fewer chances he takes with hazards that could cost strokes.

Lee Trevino, speaking of strategy, says it can all be summarized in one word: "placement". He contends that placement is always more important than distance.(6) Good golfers play for "position". That is where Hogan was a genius. He was almost always in position.

In golf each shot determines the next. The tee shot is the opening maneuver on any hole. From then on it is an attempt to get in position for as clear a shot at the green as possible. Tommy Armour stresses in his book over and over, "Play the shot that makes the next shot easy." He advised that before each shot one should take a mental survey of the situation and determine the best way to play that particular shot so that the next shot will be easy. "One of the first lessons a man or woman should learn about golfing tactics," according to Armour, "is that when it is going to take two shots to make the green, make both easy shots." (7)

All this means that the one who thinks his way around the golf course has a plan for each shot. Casper says, "Spend your time planning a shot, not worrying about it." The good golfer figures what is needed, what the risks are, what manner of shot will be the most effective, what club will be most likely to produce it, then he makes a decision. They never hit a "wish" shot. That is the opposite of thinking one's way around the golf course. They always hit a planned shot and hit it decisively. As Bruce Devlin says, you must think out **every** shot intelligently.

Cary Middlecoff said one reason for the success of Gary Player is he never hits a foolish shot.

Julius Boros said, "There are undoubtedly many angles to the psychological side of golf and probably most folks have their own theories. I have just one big simple one that I want to share with you. **Never beat yourself.**"(8)

In order not to beat oneself one must plan so he will keep the ball in play, play away from trouble, play for position so that the next shot will be easy, have a plan for each shot, think it out intelligently and play it decisively and he will be playing with good strategy and management.

(1) Palmer: *Situation Golf,* Saturday Review Press, 1972.

(2) cf Middlecoff: *Advanced Golf,* Prentice Hall, 1957, p. 98.

(3) cf Armour: *ABC's of Golf,* Simon and Schuster, 1967, p. 87.

(4) cf Boros: *How to Play Golf With an Effortless Swing,* Prentice Hall, 1964, p. 21.

(5) Casper: *Golf Shotmaking with Billy Casper,* Doubleday, 1966, p. 9.

(6) cf Trevino: *I Can Help Your Game,* Fawcett Printing Co., 1971, p. 5.

(7) Armour: *How to Play Your Best Shot All the Time,* Simon and Schuster, 1953, p. 22, 155.

(8) Boros: Ibid., p. 24.

**Taking too many chances can result in problems like Roberto de Vincenze is trying to solve**

# 22

# Playing Bold Or Playing Safe

*The majority of good golfers advocate that one should play it safe generally, but play it bold when the occasion demands.*

There are basically two kinds of golfers in terms of an overall approach to tactics or strategy: Those who play it bold and those who play it safe or more conservatively. The former is characterized by Walter Hagen and Arnold Palmer, the latter by Ben Hogan and Billy Casper.

Who can say which is best? There is no question that Palmer's daring has won him tournaments. There is still a bronze marker in the side of a bank at Royal Birkdale where Palmer won the British Open. The ball was buried in the loose sand and dirt that characterizes all of the rough of England's seaside courses. He was advised he could declare it unplayable, take a penalty and have a clear shot at the green. He asked his caddy for a club and told the gallery to get out of the way. He dug it out, dirt and all, landed on the green, sank the putt for a birdie. The plaque simply says, "Where Arnold Palmer won the British Open."

At times such an approach to the game has caused him trouble. In the 1966 U.S. Open when he had the dramatic

**Playing safe may avoid problems such as Bruce Crampton faced here**

battle with Billy Casper, he hooked into the rough on the 15th hole. He attempted to gamble with a 3 iron, but only got 75 yards, remaining in the rough. The two men tied and Palmer lost in a playoff. Those who favor playing safe point out that a more conservative choice of clubs could well have saved a stroke and the title.

Many people were critical of Casper's conservative decision in the '69 Masters to lay up on the par 5's instead of going for the green and trying for birds. He came in second. He was close enough that he might have won. However, the next year he played his usual safe game and did win.

Johnny Miller entered the select circle as a winner of one of the "big four" when he shot a record breaking 63 at Oakmont to win the 1973 Open. He had a chance to enter that select group a couple of years earlier at the Masters when he took a chance on the last day and lost. It happened this way. He was leading Charley Coody by one shot when he came to the par-3 16th. The flag was set to the back near a trap. Hoping to add to his lead, he decided to go for the pin—that was a mistake. He went into the sand, came out with a bogey and lost his lead, and, as it turned out, the tournament as well. A few minutes later Coody birdied the hole which meant a two stroke swing on the one hole. Miller lost the tournament by two strokes. Miller admitted later it was a bad percentage shot. He should have played it safe to the center of the green. He would have had a sure par and a possible bird. If he had played it safe and got his par he would have still been tied for the lead, even though Coody birdied. He gambled and lost.

Bruce Devlin, on the other hand, says he feels one should attack every hole. He takes his position with those who play it bold. He illustrates how it paid off for him in the Victorian Open at Melbourne, Australia. He intentionally hit into sand traps in two successive holes. On the 16th he felt his chances for holding the green were remote and on the 17th he was in the trees and the best way he could get close to the pin was in the sand. In both cases he splashed out and one-putted. That takes confidence. He played it bold and won.[1]

Even Devlin says one should not gamble for small stakes unless one has a reasonable chance of pulling it off. Bobby Jones used to say that one of the things that amazed him about even good golfers was the fact they would attempt shots they should have known were impossible.[2] Ben Hogan once said he had seen amateurs who would try to hit a ball through a knot hole. Jimmy Demaret said he was amazed at the way amateurs would take such chances. He said many amateurs seem to think golf is one part putting and two parts tiger hunt.

There is no question that the majority of experts advocate not taking chances unless it is absolutely necessary. Bobby

Nichols says the best advice he can give the amateur is complete in three words, "Play it safe".[3]

We referred to Palmer earlier in the chapter as one who had the reputation for playing it bold, and who tends to gamble. He disagrees. In a recent publication he said, "But one thing most people don't know about me is that I don't gamble in golf. I have never tried a difficult shot I wasn't pretty certain I could make."[4] He admitted that sometimes the shot didn't come off, but contends it was not because he gambled and lost but because he didn't hit the shot properly.

It is as much a matter of temperament as anything else. Some play better one way, some another. The real secret is to know when to play it safe and when to gamble. Gary Player says unless he needs a spectacular shot to win a tournament, he will not gamble unless the odds are in his favor.

Obviously the experts disagree. Some like it bold, some like it safe. Some have been successful playing it bold. Some have been successful playing it safe. They do agree one should not take chances unless there is a reasonable degree of confidence that it can be pulled off successfully. Whichever way they play themselves, there is no doubt about their advice to others.

(1) cf Devlin: *Play Like the Devil,* Doubleday, 1970, p. 117.

(2) cf Middlecoff: *The Golf Swing,* Prentice Hall, 1969, p. 16.

(3) cf Nichols: *Never Say Never,* Fleet Publishing Co., 1965, p. 16.

(4) Palmer: *Situation Golf,* Saturday Review Press, p. 7.

# 23

# Play The Golf Course Not The Opponent

*Most successful golfers agree that one should play the golf course and not the opponent.*

The great Harry Vardon used to say, "Treat your adversary with all due respect–as a nonentity." He said, no matter what "brilliant achievements he may accomplish, go on quietly playing your own game."(1) Most good golfers would agree.

In the 1952 Open at Dallas Julius Boros entered the final round with a two stroke lead over the field. His nearest challenger was none other than Ben Hogan who had won the year before at Oakland Hills. At one time some of his friends wanted to tell him what Hogan was doing. He said he didn't want to know. He had set his own goals and his own plan in accordance with the golf course. He knew if he got to playing the other person's game, Hogan's or anyone else's, he couldn't play his own. He kept on playing the golf course and won.

When Don January and Don Massengale met in the playoff for the P.G.A. title in 1967, January said he wasn't playing

Julius Boros just goes on playing his own game

Massengale, he was playing the golf course. He knew he had to have a seventy to win, and did.

Al Geiberger is a good example of one who plays the golf course. In the 1966 P.G.A. which he won he had a good lead in the last round when Arnold Palmer made one of his patented charges. Palmer, commenting on it, afterward said, "He has a good temperament and plays the course. He never bothers about anyone. . .I made a charge, finished second by four, and he didn't even know I was in the tournament." Of course Geiberger knew Palmer was in the tournament but he kept on playing the golf course and maintained his composure.

Bob Jones said that even in match play, he played the course not his opponent. He said he never thought of and hardly knew what the other man was doing. He knew if he played against par he would usually come out all right.

In the final round of the Greater Greensboro Open in 1971 Pete Brown, one of the better black players on the tour, was contesting for the lead when he came to the 17th tee. He looked at the scoreboard and saw that he was one shot behind. Thinking he needed a birdie to tie, he hit a good drive which left him only a short iron to the green. The pin was cut real close to a bunker on the left. Hoping for that birdie he tried for the pin, was a few inches short and ended up in the edge of the trap. The result–a bogey. The problem was–the scoreboard was wrong. He actually was tied for the lead and didn't know it. If he had known he would have played it quite differently. If he had only played the hole as he would normally have played it, he would probably have had a par, and possibly a birdie. Because of the bogey he missed by one shot. He commented afterward that he shouldn't have looked at the scoreboard anyway. If he'd played the course instead of the scoreboard he would have forced it into a playoff and he might have won.

Lee Trevino once said, "You'll never catch me playing against my opponent. . .I play against the course."

In almost any other sport from football to chess one's opponent can disrupt one's plans and nullify his preparation. By some unusual formation, some unexpected strategy he can force one to abandon his game plan–but not in golf. As the saying goes, "It's just you and the golf course."

There are exceptions, especially in match play, where a knowledge of an opponent's score is necessary, and where it may determine one's strategy, but none other than Bobby Jones, who played plenty of match tournaments said that even here it should be the exception. "After all," he said, "it's Old Man par and you whether you're playing match or medal," which is just another way of saying play the golf course and not your opponent.

Cary Middlecoff summarized the thinking of most successful golfers when he said the main opponent is really the golf course. In his words, "If you play the course intelligently you needn't worry about the opposition."(2)

Sam Snead presents a minority report on this matter of playing the golf course, not the opponent. In an article entitled "How to Read and Wreck Your Opponent" he says it is just as important to evaluate your opponent as it is the golf course. While he recognizes golf is a game for gentlemen and it is unfair to intentionally upset an opponent (although a few do), at the same time he says, if you can recognize tenseness, or that pressure is getting to him, it increases your own confidence. By playing steadier than ever you can increase your advantage. He cites several signs that indicate pressure in one's opponent: enlarging the pupils of the eyes, whiteness around the mouth, increasing the number of waggles, increasing the pace in walking, taking extra time in lining up a putt, all are indications of tension. At such times he says one should slow down and relax. Whenever an opponent begins to throw clubs, stamp his feet, or do anything that indicates temper, one should settle down, take it easy, play safe and put on more pressure. Incidentally, he does not say what one should do if the opponent is reading you.[3]

Recognizing the effectiveness of what he says, most pros would say to keep your attention on the golf course, not on your opponent.

(1) Scott: *Secrets of the Golfing Great,* A. S. Barnes, 1965, p. 147.

(2) Middlecoff: *Masters Guide to Golf,* Prentice Hall, 1960, p. 106.

(3) *Golf Digest,* April, 1970, p. 36.

# 24

# Perseverance Over Discouragement

*Most achievements are largely a victory of persistence and perseverance.*

The story is frequently told that when Edison was working on the incandescent light he tried over 700 experiments which failed. When a lab assistant became discouraged about so many failures Edison is reported to have said, "We have no failures; we know 700 things that won't work." The story may be fictional but it describes the kind of persistence that is in the background of most achievement.

George Bernard Shaw set out to be a writer. He received rejection slip after rejection slip, but he determined to write 5000 words a day whether anyone would read them or not. Such illustrations could be multiplied. The success of such persons is due not only to their brilliance, but also to their perseverance, to their capacity to continue in spite of discouragement.

Golf is no exception. Most of the great golfers, with the possible exception of Jack Nicklaus, experienced periods of discouragement before they experienced success. Even Nicklaus admitted in an article in *Sports Illustrated* that when he

**Byron Nelson, winner of eleven straight, an unmatched record, was once discouraged about his game.**

lost the Masters in 1964, after he had set his heart on winning it two years in a row, the let-down that followed ruined his whole year.

Byron Nelson has one of the most amazing records in the history of golf. His feat of winning eleven straight tournaments will probably never be duplicated. We are well aware of the old cliche that records are made to be broken—even those that have stood for a long time. This is usually true. Even Babe Ruth's record of 714 home runs was finally beaten by Henry Aaron. People said no one would ever break Ty Cobb's record of stolen bases, especially in these days of the lively ball, but Maury Wills did it. Authorities said no one would ever broad jump twenty-five feet, but in the Mexico Olympics Bob Beaman jumped over 29. The four minute mile was once considered unattainable until Roger Bannister ran it, then everybody began to do it. People used to say Hogan's records in the Masters and the Open were out of reach but Jack Nicklaus broke them both.

The thought that anyone can ever again win eleven straight tournaments in a row, however, does seem unattainable. There are so many good players on the tour today, anyone of which is capable of putting four rounds together, it is hard to see how anyone can ever dominate the game to that extent again. We feel safe in saying that this is one record that will stand. One thing is certain: if anyone ever does break it, he'll be the richest man in sports.

The famous streak was not all of Nelson's accomplishments. He won 39 other tournaments, fifty in all. He was the leading money winner in 1944 and 1945. In 1944 he won 15% of all the money offered and in 1945 he won 12%. Today the leading money winner controls about 3%. The year he won eleven straight he won eighteen tournaments in all and was second seven times. Some discount the streak because they were war years but Nelson points out he was competing against such men as Snead, Demaret, Shute, Picard, Revolta, etc. They were no pushovers. During the streak he averaged 67.45. That might not win eleven straight today, but it would win a bunch. Billy Casper won the Vardon trophy in 1968 with an average of 68.82.

Such overall excellence over a season has never been approached and will probably never be surpassed. Bobby Jones said, "At my best I never came close to the golf Nelson shoots." Tommy Armour once called him the finest golfer he had ever seen.

It is hard to believe that anyone with such a record and with such amazing consistency was ever discouraged or tempted to give up the game. One wonders what he could be discouraged about. He was in the money in 87 consecutive tournaments.

There was a time when he was both discouraged and frustrated. He bought numerous sets of clubs, which he couldn't afford, until his wife suggested that maybe it wasn't his clubs but him. After a very poor 317 in the 1935 Open he said he faced just two alternatives. One was quit the game entirely, and the other was to start an intensive study both of himself and the game of golf. He obviously chose the latter and began a program of study and self improvement that lasted five years.

He quit tinkering with his clubs and his frantic and confused practice. Instead he said he let the club makers worry about the clubs and he began a program of study and experimentation that resulted in a literal transformation of his game. He analyzed all the successful golfers of his day and appropriated the things they had in common to his own game. These efforts continued for five years but they paid off.

He won the Metropolitan Open as a virtual unknown in 1935 with a 283. This was the lowest score he had ever recorded and it paid him first prize of $750.00. At the time he had exactly $5.00 in his pocket.

More important than the money was the lift it gave his confidence. His exhaustive study of the game and his careful analysis of the methods of others gave him a thorough-going knowledge of both the fundamentals and the subtleties of the game, a knowledge he still utilizes on telecasts of golf tournaments and in magazine articles.

His endless hours on the practice tee gave him a consistency almost unequaled, then or now. For years he had trouble with his driver; in fact, he used a three wood from the tee for a long time because of it. During the streak he went 94 holes without missing a fairway. There is a story about Nelson which we assume is apocryphal that during a practice session his caddy lost a ball in the sun and was knocked down. Nelson hit him three more times before he got up.

His swing has been studied, analyzed and copied. Many things have been listed as contributing to his success. Many say it is his long irons. He said he felt it was when he developed a one piece swing, starting the clubhead, hands and shoulders back in one motion and keeping the back of his left hand square to the hole in the hitting area. Recognizing the truth of such mechanical things, the fact remains that his record would never have been attained without the perseverence he maintained throughout a long period of development and discouragement.

What was true of Nelson has been true to some degree with most of the winners. Hogan went through a period when he hardly made enough money to get from one week to the next. Bruce Devlin had trouble with varicose veins when he began the tour. He couldn't sleep because of the pain until an operation corrected it. He came in second nine times in 15 months. Such a series of near misses was most discouraging but he kept on.

There are many factors that contribute to winning golf—a good swing, mastery of the fundamentals, etc., etc., etc. Perseverence in the face of discouragement is equally important.

# 25

# Lessons From A Pro: The Royal Road To Improvement

*Good golfers are in common agreement: If you want to improve, seek the help of a pro.*

Most of the outstanding golfers are indebted to some teacher who grounded them in the fundamentals and helped to mold their game. There are a few notable exceptions such as Sam Snead, who never had a lesson in his life, but Sam Snead was a fantastic athlete with natural coordination that borders on the phenomenal. Hogan and Nelson did not have the benefit of expert instruction when they were young. They picked up their knowledge around the pro shops of Fort Worth, but each of them made a thorough-going study of the great golfers of their day and did endless experimentation in order to find out for themselves what was and was not effective.

The super stars of recent years have usually had the benefit of individual instruction. Arnold Palmer found it right at home. His father was a golf pro and began giving him instructions on cut-down golf clubs almost as soon as he went to school. Julius Boros had the great Tommy Armour to guide him. Gardner Dickinson was a protege of Ben Hogan. Bob

Goalby worked with Johnny Revolta. Jack Nicklaus credits much of his success to Jack Grout, who was the home pro at Scioto Country Club in Columbus, Ohio. He began with Grout when he was eleven years old. He still goes back to check things out with him from time to time. In fact at the start of each season he has a session or two with Grout. They begin with the grip, the stance, and go right on through the fundamentals.(1)

Good golfers recognize the value of good instruction and seek it whenever they can. Henry Ransom, golf coach at Texas A&M, has been influential in the development of many fine golfers, including Cary Middlecoff, Bobby Nichols, Paul Harney, Bill Collins and Johnny Pott. Paul Runyan, another great teacher, helped Chuck Courtney, Phil Rodgers and Gene Littler. A frequent sight at Ridglea Country Club in Fort Worth is Raymond Gafford on the practice tee with Charles Coody, Don Massengale or Jack Montgomery. When they need something checked out they come back to Fort Worth and work with Raymond.

Some golfers are known for their skill in diagnosing and analyzing a swing so they can detect a flaw even in the swing of experts. Byron Nelson and Bob Toski, for example, are frequently consulted by champions.

Harvey Penick, of the Austin Country Club in Austin, Texas, is recognized as a great teacher. Professionals on the tour call, write, and wire, seeking help. He tells them to come by, and they do—George Knudson, Dave Marr, Wes Ellis, Terry Dill, Don Massengale and Billy Maxwell are a few of those who have sought his services. George Knudson put it this way, "If something happens to my game, Harvey's the one I want to see. I wouldn't disagree with anything he says."

An article on Penick in *Golf* magazine pointed out that he never takes a negative stance. He never points out what is wrong. He always says, "You'll do better this way. . .", or "I notice the good players do it this way." (2)

In addition to such famous instructors, the touring pros frequently help each other. They know each other's game so well they can spot a change almost instantly. Gardner Dickinson is recognized as one of the best instructors on the tour and is frequently sought out for help. Strangely enough, they help each other, knowing it may be money out of their own pockets. During the practice rounds for the 1971 P.G.A. Deane Beaman noticed a slight change in Nicklaus' putting stroke. He told him about it during a bridge game. Nicklaus practiced it on the lawn that evening and won the tournament. During the 1970 Colonial in Fort Worth Homero Blancas was having trouble with his driving. Lee Trevino gave him a lesson the morning of the last round. That afternoon Blancas drove beautifully and beat Trevino by one stroke. Trevino's comment was what one would expect, "A $25,000 lesson!!"

Even Bobby Jones, with his flawless swing, had times he needed to consult the pro. In his case it was Stewart Maiden of his home course in Atlanta. A bit of Jones lore that is frequently repeated goes back to 1925 just before the National Open at Worcester, Massachusetts. Jones was having trouble but wasn't sure of the cause. Somewhat in desperation Jones called Maiden in Atlanta.

Maiden took a train at once (this was before air travel was so common), traveled to Massachusetts and watched Jones as he worked on the practice tee. After awhile he said, "Why don't you hit it on your backswing?" and walked away.

Jones was rushing his backswing and throwing himself off balance ever so slightly. But he couldn't see himself. Even though he was the best player in the world at the time he needed a professional to help him out.

The experts are pretty much in common agreement. The two most important factors necessary to improve a golf game are lessons from a competent pro and practice. The two go together. It does little good to take lessons unless a person is going to practice what he's taught. To take a lesson and expect one's game to improve without practice is to ask too much. Tommy Armour said that one should practice four hours for each lesson. To practice without lessons may do as much harm as good. A person may only solidify his faults. Practice under the direction of a pro provides maximum efficiency. (See section on Practice.)

The beginner should seek the help of a pro until he has the fundamentals thoroughly ingrained into his game. The more advanced player may seek a pro when he is in a slump, when he needs help on a specific shot or a specific club, or just to check out his game in general.

If one would play "smart golf" one of the smartest things he can do is find a good teaching pro and get his help.

(1) cf Nicklaus: *Golf My Way,* Simon and Schuster, 1974, p. 198.

(2) cf Trinkle: *Golf Magazine,* April, 1971, p. 52.

**Teaching pro Roland Harper of Colonial Country Club in Fort Worth, with Charley Coody former TCU player and Masters Champion**

**Gardner Dickinson receives congratulations from his former teacher Ben Hogan on winning at Colonial**

# 26

# Smarter Practice Means Lower Scores

*All good golfers agree: what happens on the golf course is directly proportional to what happens on the practice tee and on the putting green.*

Bobby Nichols, who won $60,000.00 in one tournament (the largest single purse ever offered at that time, 1970), says there is only one way to become a steady winner at golf, "You have to become oblivious to everything else but your game, practice until you're ready to drop and learn to concentrate without letup."

Probably no one else has ever demonstrated the truth of such a statement more than Gary Player. Gary Player, while still a young pro in South Africa, set as his goal the winning of all four of the major tournaments, commonly referred to as the "grand slam". Only two men had done it before, Gene Sarazen and Ben Hogan. Player completed his grand slam when he won the U.S. Open in 1965. Nicklaus has completed it since, in fact he has done it twice. Three others have come close. Nelson won all but the British Open, Snead has won them all but the U.S. Open, and Palmer has won them all but the P.G.A.

Player's record is all the more remarkable when one considers how small he is. He not only competes with men much taller and heavier in a day when golf courses give an advantage to the power hitters, but he defeats them as well. Bellrive, where he won the Open measured 7191 yards, the longest course in the history of the Open. The predictions before the tournament were that only the power hitters had a chance. Player proved that accuracy as well as brute strength is important, even on longer courses. He beat Kel Nagle in a playoff for the title and gave his entire purse to charity.

Player didn't get much encouragement from other professionals when he began his career. They said his swing was too flat, he couldn't chip, and he was too small. Such statements only increased his determination to try harder. He was well aware of his limitations.

He began one of the most rigorous, extensive, exhaustive, thorough-going programs of preparation ever attempted by any golfer. Player once said that no one has enough natural ability to be a champion. It is far too demanding for that. Natural ability must be present to be sure, but it is developed by careful, intelligent, persistent practice.

He began his practice program when he was still a small boy in South Africa. He would literally practice all day, beginning early in the morning, pausing only for lunch and a nap, then returning to the practice tee for an afternoon session.

He would work for hours on a single shot such as an intentional hook or slice, or with one club such as the driver or the wedge. He not only practiced from regular lies such as is found on the typical practice area, but he would practice from the rough, from bad lies, and from the sand. In other words he practiced every conceivable situation he might face on the golf course. He would practice these unusual situations not only occasionally but continuously until he was convinced of the results.

He has frequently told how he would set a goal of holing out five shots from a sand trap and stay until he'd done it even though it took two or three hours. He would do the same with chipping, resolving not to leave until he'd holed out at least ten chip shots from off the green.

He even practiced in bad weather although he warns that practicing in pouring down rain, such as he did, or in strong winds could alter one's swing and create bad habits.

He maintained his motivation for practice by reminding himself of his goals. Even when he was just beginning he had his eye on the "big four" and would say to himself "this shot is for the United States Open", or "this shot is for the British Open". He would putt two or three balls pretending one was Hogan's, one was Snead's and one was his own and that they were playing in a big tournament.

Such rigorous practice produced results. It was in these lengthy sessions he gained a mastery of the fundamentals. He has always contended that the fundamentals are made secure on the practice tee. Today he is recognized as one of the best shot makers in the game. Only he knows the hours of practice and the sore hands and muscles that made his swing appear so natural and his mastery of all the shots so reliable and dependable.

Player contends that, except for Ben Hogan, he has practiced longer and harder than any other golfer. That well may be true.

Hogan is another example "par excellance." He practiced until he wore blisters on his hands. During his early days on the tour after he had finished a round he would usually go to the practice tee for a lengthy session. Then he would take a club to his hotel room and study his backswing plane in a mirror, trying to memorize it so he could develop a swing that would repeat. He would also take his putter to his room and practice on the carpet. When he won the Portland Open with a record breaking 261, 19 under par, he was seen out practicing again early the next morning.

A story which Hogan tells is a case in point. "However, having worked hard on my golf with all the mentality and all the physical resources available to me, I have managed to play some very good shots at very important stages of major tournaments. To cite one example, which many of my friends remember with particular fondness—and I, too, for that matter—in 1950 at Merion, I needed to hit an elusive, well-trapped, slightly plateaued green from about 200 yards out. There are easier shots in golf. I went with a two-iron and played what was in my honest judgment one of the best shots of my last round, perhaps one of the best I played during the tournament. The ball took off on a line for the left center of the green, held its line firmly, bounced on the front edge of the green. . .It was all I could have asked for. . .

"I bring up this incident. . .because I have discovered in many conversations that the view I take of this shot (and others like it) is markedly different from the view most spectators seem to have formed. They are inclined to glamourize the actual shot. . .They tend to think of it as something unique in itself, something almost inspired, you might say. . . I don't see it that way at all. I didn't hit that shot then. . . that late afternoon at Merion. I'd been practicing that shot since I was 12 years old."(1)

Hogan and Player both continue to practice. Before he won the World Match Play at Piccadily, England in 1971 where they played 36 holes a day, Player ate a quick lunch so he could practice between rounds. He said he had hit as many balls as could be hit in three weeks. In addition to practicing between rounds, he would hit balls after the round until his caddy couldn't see to follow the flight of the ball. Any day at Shady Oaks Country Club in Fort Worth Hogan can be seen hitting hundreds of balls to a caddy just as he did when he was known as "the hawk" and was competing regularly on the tour. In fact Hogan was recently quoted as saying he would rather practice than play because it is more fun.

Few have put forth the efforts or practiced like Player and Hogan but similar stories could be told about most of the successful golfers. George Knudson used to spend six to eight hours a day just practicing. Doug Ford was troubled by a hook early in his career. He went through the tedious routine of practicing a slice almost daily for three months, but he controlled the hook and became a good slicer. Billy Casper practiced putting by the hour. In fact he often practiced into the dark. Some feel this is one way he developed his marvelous touch. When Lee Trevino entered the British Open in 1970 he practiced with the English ball, hitting over 700 shots a day just to get used to it.

All the pros agree—it is practice that develops one's game. They also agree on certain principles of practice. Practice should be combined with lessons. Practice without guidance may only solidify one's faults. Practice under the direction of a pro provides maximum efficiency.

Just hitting golf balls isn't practice. It may be good exercise but it doesn't lead to improvement. Palmer says when one is practicing he should take his time, check the grip, reconsider the fundamentals and have a plan for each shot.[2]

Gary Player says every session should have a goal, a definite purpose. It may be improvement in the use of one club, or one aspect of the swing. Many pros advocate concentrating on one facet of the swing during a practice session, a slow back swing, a high follow-through, delaying releasing of the hands, or any other important fundamental.

Nicklaus says that he practices to get the feel of the club. This would be similar to the advice of Ernest Jones the great teacher. He says one should practice constantly to "focus. . . attention on the feel of the swinging action of the clubhead." When one gets this sense of feel in practice, he says, he can rely on it in competition.[3]

Most pros agree that one should always aim at a target. There may be exceptions when one is only attempting to make a good contact but on the golf course one has a target in mind. He should do the same in practice.

They also say you should never rush your practice. Hitting one ball right after another only spoils one's timing. This isn't the way one plays. Player says he leaves his pile of balls a bit behind him so he has to go after one between shots.

Sam Snead says one should practice his weaknesses. He

advocates listing them on paper, then practicing to eliminate them. He says if one will do this for a few months it will do as much to improve his efficiency as any other procedure. Hogan used to take a note book to the practice tee and record his experience.

There are differences of opinion about which clubs or shots should receive the most attention. Bobby Nichols says that since woods and putts comprise 80% of a round, they should receive most of the practice time. Casper says since the short game is so important for scoring, it should receive at least 50% of one's practice time. Harvey Penick, who Byron Nelson says is one of the best teaching pros in the business, advises one should practice mainly with the 5, 6, and 7 irons.

Most of them agree that one should practice from the sand, from the rough, and from difficult lies, something most players neglect, and that putting should receive a major portion of one's practice time. They also say don't practice when you are tired or have lost interest; it only leads to bad habits.

According to the experts two things lead to improvement in golf—practice and see your pro, or vice versa.

(1) Hogan: *The Modern Fundamentals of Golf,* A. S. Barnes, 1957, p. 13 & 14.

(2) cf Palmer: *My Game and Yours,* Simon and Schuster, 1963, p. 50.

(3) Jones: *Swing the Clubhead,* Dodd Mead and Co., 1957, p. 116.

# 27

# Training And Conditioning

*One plays better golf if he is in condition to do so.*

An article in a golf magazine entitled "Conditioning for Your Game" has a sub title which reads, "You play better and think better if you're in good physical condition."[1] This statement would receive few arguments in theory. It is also recognized that many players with excellent ability do not go through the discipline necessary to keep in top condition. In fact some have been criticized for their neglect of conditioning. Some articles in the press have objected to calling the golfers "athletes" because so many are overweight and make little effort to train or stay in condition.

Gary Player is the exception. He probably is more rigorous about physical conditioning than any of the top names of golf. He is only five feet seven inches and weighs only about 150 pounds. He recognized very early that if he was to compete with men who were taller and heavier than he was he would have to follow a program of rigorous exercise. He ran to build up his legs. He did push-ups to build up his arms. He used to do 80 finger-tip push-ups a day but stopped when he found his chest and shoulder muscles were beginning to tight-

Tommy Bolt looks fit after many years on the tour

Gary Player is little but is able to compete with much larger and stronger men

en and restrict a free swing. To build up his back muscles, wrist and forearms he lifted weights. He learned special exercises with the weights to improve the body turn and foot work.

He is also very careful about his rest and food. He is something of a food fadist. He avoids fried foods, resists desserts, and keeps his weight at a good playing limit. He even uses Yoga and finds it helps him to relax.

In spite of all this, in 1960 he found he wasn't reaching the par 5's at Augusta in two. He talked to Peter Thompson, of Australia, an excellent shot maker (four times winner of the British Open, but not a long hitter). Thompson said he didn't think he could ever win the Masters because he couldn't carry the water on some of the par 5's. Player determined that wouldn't happen to him. He began to work with professional body-builders; he hired his own trainer; he intensified his exercises, concentrating on push-ups and the weights. The next year he carried the 5's and won the Masters.

In spite of his great success, even in the midst of constant travel and during competition he maintains his rigid diet, careful rest and continuous exercise. Some people advised him against exercise during competition, but he says he enjoys it so much he doesn't want to give it up, even during competition.

He feels that running is the best single exercise there is, although jumping rope has the advantage that it uses the hands as well as the legs.

There is no question in Player's mind that his conditioning program has been helpful in his golf. It not only has added distance to his tee shots, and makes him more effective in heavy rough but eliminates fatigue as well. In a newspaper interview he said, "At the pace we live today, a body can take just so much. That's why I believe the better physical condition you're in, the better you can combat strain."(2)

Tommy Bolt contends that golfers are athletes and that they must be in good condition to play well. He points out that they have to hike five miles a day, uphill and downhill, in all kinds of weather, as well as spend hours on the practice tee in addition to continued mental pressure. He contends that to do this for ten months a year requires that he be in good physical condition or he "will get cut off the team." The ones who cut him won't be a coach or a trainer. He is his own coach and trainer. It will be the other golfers who did stay in shape.(3)

A major topic in any discussion of conditioning is diet and weight. Here there are two outstanding examples in recent years, Billy Casper and Jack Nicklaus. Both lost considerable weight, and both emphasized the psychological factor of discipline and the accompanying satisfaction that such an achievement gives.

Billy Casper began his diet because of an allergy problem. When he found that he was allergic to most common foods he went on a bizarre diet of buffalo meat, whale meat, and a long list of unusual items faithfully reported and embellished in the sports pages. The first item obviously led to the nickname "Buffalo Bill." The result was not only freedom from allergy problems but the loss of weight. Between the Open which he won in 1959 and the Open that he won in 1966 he lost forty pounds. Those who saw him on the course or on television before and after the diet could hardly believe it was the same person.

The result was not only an improved appearance but a better swing and a better stamina as well. There was another intangible that accompanied this achievement. Casper, speaking of the diet, said, "Beyond that, as anyone who has ever dieted seriously will agree, you get a certain respect for yourself and pride in your self-control." (4)

Jack Nicklaus weighed about 220 pounds when he won his first Masters in 1963. The day he was interviewed for *"Golf and Club"* magazine in 1971 he weighed 188 pounds. He said he began his diet because of a fatigue factor. Like Casper he spoke of the satisfaction that comes from a disciplined effort.

His description of his experience was as follows. "I had to discipline myself during the period when I lost weight and I came right back after that and won the first two tournaments I played in. I think anytime anybody disciplines himself he is proud of what he's done and it carries over in other things—it makes him do other things better. The only reason I wanted to lose weight was because I was starting to get tired near the end of tournaments. I had never before gotten tired in my life."(5)

In his book *Golf My Way* published some three or four years later he said that the most value he received from the experience was it made him feel better physically and mentally.(6)

Many golfers do exercises to keep the hands and wrists in condition. Ben Hogan used to squeeze rubber balls. Julius Boros advocates the same thing plus gripping and regripping a club around the house. Jimmy Thomson, in addition to squeezing rubber balls, advocates isometrics consisting of putting the points of the fingers against each other and pushing at maximum strength. Tom Nieporte advocates winding a piece of clothes line rope around a wooden handle and then drawing a weighted object up from the ground by turning the handle. This strengthens the hands and wrists. Many utilize hand grippers and other prepared instruments for such purposes.

Articles appear regularly in the golf journals listing isometrics and isotonic exercises that are designed to keep the golf muscles in condition. One book has been published which lists the exercises used by many of the world's best golfers, both professional and amateur. Some of the more common and frequently used ones are pressing the face of a club against an immovable object and pushing on the handle with maximum strength for ten seconds. Placing a club behind the back and in the crooks of the elbows and bending from side to side. Some advocate standing with the feet together and swinging a five iron. Such an exercise increases both balance and body turn.(7)

Gene Sarazen says the best single conditioning exercise is swinging a weighted club 40 or 50 times a day. These can be purchased commercially or can be made by weighting the head of an old driver. Lacking a weighted club, a rake or a hoe will do. It increases the strength of the hands, improves balance, tempo and timing. Sarazen kept several such clubs in different places all over the house and farm and would swing one of them whenever the opportunity presented itself. He dates the improvement of his own game to the time he began this practice.[8] Tom Nieporte, Dave Marr and several others have benefited from this practice too. In fact conditioning is probably important whether one plays golf or not. A generation ago it was no problem. We were a rural society and everyone had enough exercise to keep healthy. This is no longer true. If golf serves to keep one in condition it is performing an added service.

(1) *Golf and Club,* April, 1971, p. 38.

(2) *Fort Worth Star Telegram, May 22, 1971.*

(2) Fort Worth Star-Telegram, May 22, 1971.

(3) cf *The Hole Truth*, by Tommy Bolt with Jimmy Mann. Copyright 1971, J. B. Lippincott Co.

(4) *Golf Digest,* June, 1967, p. 36.

(5) *Golf and Club,* April, 1971, p. 29.

(6) cf Nicklaus: *Golf My Way,* Simon and Schuster, 1974, p. 193.

(7) cf Zanger (ed): *Exercises for Better Golf,* Nelson and Sons, 1965.

(8) cf Sarazen: *Better Golf After Forty,* Harper and Row, 1967, p. 35.

# 28

# Courtesy, Sportsmanship And Fair Play

*Golf is a game of gentlemen (and ladies).*

In these days of violence that is reflected even in sports, golf remains a game for gentlemen. This is true of both spectators and participants alike. The crowds at football and basketball games, hockey matches and baseball games make every effort to disrupt and distract the opposition. This is considered part of the game. A baseball game without at least one leather-lunged fan taunting the opposition would seem pretty dull. Boos, insults, shouting during a tense moment are expected.

Not so in golf. The galleries surrounding a green during a tense moment can be amazingly quiet. There have been a few incidents that have been unpleasant, to be sure, but they are the exception. In the early days of Nicklaus' career, when some of Palmer's most ardent fans couldn't accept the fact that he was challenging their idol, they were known to cheer a bad shot; and the black players have been subject to some indignities, but even these represent individuals not the crowd.

The players have almost always been able to maintain their

own poise and courtesy in the presence of such incidents. Once when Lee Elder, the talented young black player, hit a particularly good shot, a man in the crowd said, "What did you hit on that shot, boy?" Elder's reply was characteristic, "I hit a five iron, sir."

He expressed his own attitude after the round. "People like this are in a small minority. If I lower myself to his level it will do more harm than good. So I keep my mouth shut. . .It's going to get better."

Lee Elder continues to swing

In spite of such occasional incidents golf is chacterized by courtesy on the part of galleries and fair play on the part of participants. In the main they serve as their own referees and umpires.

There have been many incidents that could be recounted. Dow Finsterwald, playing in the Masters a few years ago, stroked a practice putt on the edge of the green after he had holed out. This is not an uncommon occurrence when one wants to make an adjustment in his stroke. After the round he called a two stroke penalty on himself. Arnold Palmer, playing in the British Open at Royal Birkdale, noticed that his ball moved ever so slightly in a hazard. No one noticed it. Palmer called a penalty on himself. He did the same thing in the 1972 Citrus Golf Tournament in Orlando, Florida. On the second day he hooked a shot to the left of the green. It landed in the rough. He removed a loose impediment then took a practice swing. While he was taking the practice swing the ball moved slightly. No one saw it. When he finished the round he told a P.G.A. official and a penalty was assessed. As a result he missed the cut for the first time in four years. Bruce Devlin was leading the Colonial NIT at Fort Worth when his ball landed in a fairway trap on number six. As he set his stance the ball moved. He hadn't touched it. No one saw it. He too called the penalty on himself. Fortunately both Palmer and Devlin went on to win. Unfortunately Finsterwald didn't.

Tommy Bolt tells of an incident that occurred in the Florida Open: Skip Alexander a former touring pro hit his second shot into the trees on a par five hole. They had some trouble locating the ball, but when they did he hit a fine shot through the branches onto the green. His partners congratulated him on such a good shot. He said the ball moved as he addressed it and he would have to take a penalty. His partners said, "We didn't see it move." He replied, "God saw it move," and took the penalty.(1)

Can you imagine a half-back going down the side lines and saying he had touched the line, or an outfielder saying he had trapped a fly ball? In fact, how many pitchers have admitted that on occasion they have moistened a ball, which is definitely against the rules?

The good golfers not only play honestly, they do not take unfair advantage of their opponent. A frequent sight is Palmer after holing out his putt, holding up his hand to keep his "army" from rushing to the next tee while his opponent is putting.

Nieporte and Sauer in their study of the mental side of golf point out that there are many things that can distract a player which might be called gamemanship, such as unusually slow play, conversation that would make one swing-conscious, standing too close when one is lining up a putt, etc. Their conclusion was that while such things do occur, they are usually unconscious. We hope this is true and think in the main it is.

Doug Ford contends that when one is considerate of the

other person and observes the rules he actually plays better golf. He says, "If you do something that isn't allowed by the rules (and you offend yourself as well as your fellow players when this happens), then you're bound to play for awhile in a disturbed frame of mind. . ." On the other hand, he says, if one is considerate of his opponents and plays by the rules he will be ". . .playing with a clear mind–(he'll) be thinking golf." (2)

Courtesy is important both for "your" game and "his" according to Ford. So he advises golfers to remember that "your" game is important to you and "his" game is important to him–which is something of an application of the golden rule as applied to golf.

The really good golfers have extended their courtesy and sportsmanship to their attitudes after the round is over. They can lose graciously and win with humility.

Ward Thomas, golf correspondent of the Manchester Guardian, a golf writer of the old school, refers to Nicklaus as one of the really great stars of the game. When Nicklaus was only 25 years old he said of him, "There is in this admirable young man the stuff of the fantastic, the phenomenal, the likes of which may never be seen again." (This was written long before he became the first to win the big four tournaments twice.) These are superlative terms, yet he has had a superlative record.

Commenting on his humility Ward Thomas said, "In all the time I have known him, I have seen no sign of vanity, neither have I heard him boast about his golf, his income, or anything else." Then he added, "Imagine how insufferable he might have been." (3)

Golfers are human, like everyone else, if not more so–yet the good ones as a whole demonstrate amazing courtesy, sportsmanship, fair play and humility.

(1) *The Hole Truth,* by Tommy Bolt with Jimmy Mann. Copyright 1971 by Tommy Bolt. Reprinted by permission of J. B. Lippincott Co.

(2) Ford: *Getting Started in Golf,* Cornerstone Library, 1970, p. 116.

(3) cf Wind (ed): *The Ream of Sport,* Simon and Schuster, 1968, p. 411, 412.

# 29

# Enjoy The Game

*Golf is a game: it was meant to be enjoyed.*

Richard Cabot, famous Boston physician once wrote a book called *What Men Live By*. He stated in the Introduction that when he wrote it he had in mind those persons who were sick or in trouble but needed something no medication could provide.

The book was divided into four sections. Each section had one word for a title. The four words were: Work, Play, Love and Worship. Our culture has emphasized the value of work, over-emphasized it to some extent. We don't need to be convinced of its value. Psychiatrists, psychologists, marriage counselors and poets all stress the need to love. They remind us that only he who can love and be loved is emotionally mature. Ministers and theologians speak of our need to worship—although many neglect it.

The need to play has been largely ignored. Yet play is highly important, especially in our culture of pressure, tension, stress and strain. Every man needs something that he does for the sheer pleasure of doing it, something that he does not do for profit, but for fun. Play is important for one's physical, mental and emotional health.

Golf should be fun, says the Merry Mex

The very word "game" implies that golf is meant to be enjoyed. Tommy Armour paraphrases a bit of Scripture when he says, "For what is a man profited if he sinks a 200 yard approach shot but doesn't enjoy the game."(1) The phrase that is repeated so many times each weekend in America, "Let's go play golf" implies that golf is something to be played—that is enjoyed. Granted some make work out of it, and many do not enjoy it—yet it is a game nonetheless.

George Archer was asked what was the best advice he could give to weekend golfers. He answered in two words: "Have fun."

Probably no one ever enjoyed playing golf more than Walter Hagen. His escapades are legendary. The one statement which he repeated on many occasions, and which is most often quoted in various forms, whenever reference to him and his approach to golf is made, went something like this. "Never hurry and don't worry. . .and don't forget to stop and smell the flowers on the way."

For the pros golf is strictly business. This chapter is primarily for the amateur. For him golf should be fun. However there is nothing wrong with a man enjoying his work, for that matter, and many pros do. These experts have some valuable counsel to give here also.

The first thing they would suggest is to learn to play well. We enjoy most the things we do well. All the other suggestions in this volume, the encouragement to get help from a pro, all the knowledge one can gain about the game, should help one play better and thus enjoy it more. The more one improves the more pleasure the game provides.

In fact, improvement is half the fun. Every time one sees his handicap go down a stroke or two it is a source of genuine pleasure. When one ceases to improve he loses interest. One of the beauties of golf is that no one can get so good that there isn't room for improvement.

The next suggestion they would make is to maintain reasonable expectations of oneself. This is not to contradict what is said above. One should try to improve, but within reasonable expectations. Jack Nicklaus points out that one doesn't watch a professional baseball player hit a home run and expect to duplicate it. He doesn't watch a professional football player on TV and go out and try to do the same thing himself. Yet he will watch professional golfers, who have practiced exhaustively for years, had extensive help from the best teachers, who play every day and in competition four days a week, and he expects to go out on Saturday and do the same thing.(2) The amazing thing is how close the week end golfer can emulate the pros.

They also advise, don't be too disappointed with a bad round. Even the pros have them as we saw earlier in this study. Jack Nicklaus won the Open, at an amazingly young age. He seemed unbeatable. The next year he didn't make the cut. The day this is written the papers carry the story that Arnold Palmer had a 13 on a hole. In the first twelve tournaments of 1970 Bob Shaw won twice but failed to make the cut five times. Tommy Armour who studied as many golfers as anyone, pro and amateur, said, "When are we going to realize that missing simple shots is part of being human." As we quoted Julius Boros earlier, "What if you do not knock it into the trap? Your life doesn't depend on it. Not even your living."

On some occasions the only solution is to laugh at oneself and go on. In the San Diego Open in 1969 Jack Nicklaus four putted from 30 feet. His first putt was long by about four feet. He missed the putt coming back by 12 inches. There was a slight bump in the green which he didn't see but caused his tap in to skitter along the edge. Nicklaus' comment about his last putt is worth repeating. "That fourth putt was a beauty," he said. "It went right smack in the center of the cup." (3)

In order to enjoy the game one should appreciate the good shots. Palmer says what other people find in poetry or art museums he finds in a good drive down the middle.(4) We agree it is a thing of beauty. The point is everyone hits some good shots, even on a bad day. Enjoy the good shots. They should be remembered as much as the bad ones. Reflect on them long enough and they may become habitual.

Enjoy the fringe benefits. Most golf courses are very scenic—some more than others to be sure—but they all have the sky and the clouds to see, and most of them are in a setting of natural beauty. There is a healing power in nature and we don't get enough contact with it in our urbanized society.

Exercise is good for everyone, again, especially in our sedentary culture. Walking is one of the best exercises there is. Our bodies were meant to be used and most people don't use them enough. Golf makes this both possible and enjoyable.

It is good to be with one's friends. Fellowship is important in life, it is needed in a competitive, impersonal society. All of these things are present and valuable, whether the score is good or not. Granted that one has to be rather philosophical about it, on a day when the score is not so good, but the fact remains that these things can be enjoyed.

Keep everything in perspective. Francis Ouimet, who at 20 years of age upset the great Ray and Vardon from England in a play off for the U.S. Open (1913) at Brookline once said in a speech—"To win a championship is a great personal satisfaction but after all it's only another game of golf."

One of the beauties of golf is the fact that one can immerse himself in a round, do his very best, play to win, but it's no great tragedy if he loses. He can then go back to his regular tasks, grateful for the pleasures he has had, better off for having gotten away and relaxed for awhile. He has had fun. Now he can give himself to his other tasks, with renewed effort and committment.

(1) Armour: *The ABC's of Golf,* Simon and Schuster, 1967, p. 185.

(2) cf Nicklaus: *The Greatest Game of All,* Simon and Schuster, 1969, p. 278, 279.

(3) Palmer: *Situation Golf,* Saturday Review Press, 1963, p. 10.

(4) cf Palmer: *My Game and Yours,* Simon and Schuster, 1963, p. 10.

**Determination—Jack Nicklaus sets high goals**

# 30

# Dedication And Commitment

*The great players have all been dedicated players.*

There is a certain plus factor about the great players that is hard to define. Call it desire, call it determination, call it the pursuit of excellence, call it dedication and commitment, call it what you will, it is the decisive factor that separates the good golfers from the great ones.

Tom Nieporte and Don Sauer in their study of the psychological aspects of fifty leading pros said, "The one psychological strength which all successful professional athletes seem to share is desire. . .the deep motivation to succeed which we call desire."(1) All the good golfers have had it. Vardon had it, Jones certainly had it, Nelson had it, all the great ones of the past possessed it.

There never have been so many talented golfers as there are at the present time. The ones who win consistently, who win year after year, all possess this quality. It certainly is true of the Palmers, Players, Caspers, the Nicklauses, who have dominated the game for the last decade.

In 1971 Jack Nicklaus won the P.G.A. at Palm Beach Gardens to complete the grand slam of the four major tournaments for the second time. Only three other golfers, Sarazen, Hogan and Player, had ever done it once. He wasn't satisfied. He said he wanted to surpass Bobby Jones' record of 13 major tournaments, "That's what you play for," he said, "to separate yourself from the crowd." In 1973 he did that. In 1974 he published a book entitled *Golf My Way* in which he said he felt his game was only about 75% of what his goals were. "Desire," he said, "is the most important factor in golf."(2)

In terms of desire, however, no one has ever excelled Hogan. Grantland Rice in his book on great athletes he had known listed all the great golfers he had covered as a sports writer. It included most of them up to that time, (1954) Armour, Hagen, Sarazen, Jones, etc. Then he spoke of Hogan, "Through his complete dedication to the sport, Hogan has built in himself that 'more of everything'–particularly brains–it takes to win than any golfer I ever saw."(3)

Jimmy Demaret, who probably knew Hogan as well as anybody, said, "Sure he has great skills with the clubs. So have many fine golfers. But none can surpass his determination to win; his quiet confidence that he will win; . . .his complete concentration, and his long and continuing hours of practice.

"We're all serious about golf, make no mistake about that, but Ben has a single-mindedness of purpose that makes the rest of us look like carefree school boys."

Herbert Warren Wind, noted golf writer, who collaborated with Hogan on his book, said, "It is really quite doubtful if any player throughout golf's long history has ever brought to his studies the basic tenacity, the acute and brilliantly ordered method, and the hours of relentless exploration that have marked Ben Hogan's efforts to understand the game as clearly as possible in order to be able to play it as well as possible."(4)

When Nick Seitz interviewed Hogan for an article in *Golf Digest* he asked if he thought there would ever again be one man who completely dominated the game. Hogan replied that there might be, but he paused and said, "He'll have to be an awfully dedicated man."(5)

(1) Nieporte and Sauer: *Mind Over Golf,* Doubleday, 1968, p. 12.

(2) cf Nicklaus: *Golf My Way,* Simon and Schuster, 1974, p. 254, 255.

(3) Rice: *The Tumult and The Shouting,* A. S. Barnes, 1954, p. 307.

(4) Hogan: *The Modern Fundamentals of Golf,* A. S. Barnes. 1957, Introduction.

(5) *Golf Digest,* September, 1970, p. 33.

**Success**

# In Conclusion

Let me revert to my own profession and point out a lesson that can be derived from all of this. Much that can be learned from the experts in one profession can be applied to another. Many of the lessons learned from successful golfers can be applied in other fields, some of them to life itself.

In most areas of experience it is the intangibles that count. It is sincere effort, patience and persistence, confidence and concentration, dedication and commitment that produce results.

We express our appreciation to the following authors and publishers for permission to quote from their publications.

Mr. Ben Hogan and A. S. Barnes and Company, Inc. for permission to quote from THE MODERN FUNDAMENTALS OF GOLF, by Ben Hogan © 1957. To A. S. Barnes and Company, Inc., for permission to quote from SECRETS OF THE GOLFING GREAT compiled by Tom Scott © 1965, and from THE TUMULT AND THE SHOUTING by Grantland Rice © 1954.

Doubleday & Company, Inc., for permission to quote from MIND OVER GOLF by Tom Nieporte and Don Sauers © 1968, from PLAY LIKE THE DEVIL by Bruce Devlin © 1970, and from GOLF SHOTMAKING WITH BILLY CASPER by Billy Casper © 1966 a Golf Digest Book.

Dobb, Mead & Company for permission to quote from SWING THE CLUBHEAD by Ernest Jones © 1952.

E. P. Dutton & Co., Inc. for permission to quote from SITUATION GOLF by Arnold Palmer. Copyright © 1970 by Arnold Palmer. Reprinted by permission of the publishers, Saturday Review Press.

Hart Publishing Co., Inc., for permission to quote from THE GOLF IMMORTALS by Tom Scott and Geoffrey Cousins, © 1969.

J. B. Lippincott Company for permission to quote from THE HOLE TRUTH by Tommy Bolt with Jimmy Mann. Copyright © 1971 by Tommy Bolt. Reprinted by permission of J. B. Lippincott Company.

Gary Player, Golf Marks N. V. and the McGraw-Hill Book Company for permission to quote from POSITIVE GOLF by Gary Player © 1968.

Prentice-Hall, Inc., for permission to quote from CARY MIDDLECOFF'S MASTER GUIDE TO GOLF by Cary Middlecoff © 1960, and HOW TO PLAY GOLF WITH AN EFFORTLESS SWING by Julius Boros, © 1964.

Quadrangle/the New York Times Book Co., for permission to quote from PRACTICAL GOLF by John Jacobs and Ken Bowden Copyright © 1972 by John Jacobs and Ken Bowden.

Toni Mendez, Inc., for permission to quote from SHAVING STROKES WITH FRANK BEARD by Frank Beard © 1968.

Simon & Schuster, Inc., for permission to quote from MY GAME AND YOURS by Arnold Palmer © 1963, from A ROUND OF GOLF WITH TOMMY ARMOUR by Tommy Armour © 1959, from THE ABC'S OF GOLF by Tommy Armour © 1969, from HOW TO PLAY YOUR BEST GOLF ALL THE TIME by Tommy Armour © 1961, from THE GREATEST GAME OF ALL by Jack Nicklaus © 1965.

Golf Digest for permission to quote from GOLF DIGEST magazine, issues of June © 1967, April © 1970, and April © 1972.